Parenting the Witch's Way

Raising Little Witchlings

by Amanda Wilson

First Edition, 2022

Tonya A. Brown
3436 Magazine St
#460
New Orleans, LA 70115
www.witchwaypublishing.com

Editor: Tonya A. Brown
Copy Editor: Carrie Pitzulo
Internal Design: Emily Barta
Cover Design: Tonya A. Brown
Graphics: Anna Babich

Printed in the United States of America

ISBN: Print 978-1-0880-2439-3 | eBook 978-1-0880-2442-3

For Joshua, my beloved first born son, who inspires me with his passion for life and unwavering confidence; and for Logan, my precious baby, who taught me that love makes miracles.

AcKNoWLedgMeNtS

I WANT TO EXPRESS THE IMMENSE APPRECIATION I have for Tonya Brown (author, *The Door to Witchcraft*; Editor-in-Chief, *Witch Way Magazine*; Host, *The Witch Daily Show* podcast). This book, *Raising Little Witchlings: Parenting the Witch's Way*, would not exist if it were not for Tonya. *Raising Little Witchlings* started as a monthly column in *Witch Way Magazine*, and in 2021, Tonya approached me with an offer to turn almost three years' worth of monthly articles into a book. My gratitude for Tonya goes beyond this and all the other opportunities she has offered me, though. I am both in awe of, and inspired by, her creative mind, impressive skill set, and her ability to establish and achieve goals with confidence and grace. The way she maintains balance between her responsibilities, passions, and pursuits motivates me. This book would simply not exist if it were not for that inspiration and motivation. Tonya, from the bottom of my heart, thank you.

The other person I want to thank is Jody George, the love of my life and father of my child. When life became too heavy, and the fear of failure started creeping close, his love, respect, and confidence gave me the strength and courage I needed to continue. Moreover, he sees me for who I am. He made me realize that I am worthy of being seen, and that I have purpose. I discovered that I hold within me the potential to make a positive difference in the lives of others. Knowing this enables me to relentlessly pursue my goals, fearlessly pushing past obstacles until I meet my objective. The love we share is so strong, so deep, and so rare that it has removed a veil that adversity put over my eyes, allowing me to see the vibrant magic of life. Jody, my love, for that, and so much more, thank you.

PARENTING THE WITCH'S WAY

RaiSiNG LittLe Witchlings

by AMANda WiLSON

Introduction

"A child is a seed of the future...they are our desires made manifest. They are our sacred responsibility."

—DR. HANNAH E. JOHNSTON

P ARENTING IS A JOURNEY—A BEAUTIFUL, SOUL-FULFILLING, albeit trying, journey. From the moment we find out we are expecting— whether it be pregnancy, surrogacy, or adoption—parenting becomes our life. Once the little ones arrive, we become consumed with meeting their physical and cognitive needs. We often forget that they are whole people who need just as much spiritual nourishment as we do. What better way to address these needs than to involve them in your own magical practice? We are witches, and many of us are Pagans, so our lives are intricately interwoven with our spiritual journey. Involving our children forges a deep connection with them. We establish a foundation upon which our kids will develop their own path as they grow into adulthood. Moreover, we provide for them a stable environment that is encouraging, supportive, and that prepares them for the real world.

If you are reading this book, then you have probably decided, or are trying to decide, whether or not to raise your child as a little *witchling*. Or, perhaps, you are considering starting a family and want to know what it could be like as a witch parent. Regardless of where you are on this path of parenthood, I am confident that many of your questions will be answered here. This book offers advice that is grounded in a combination of personal experience and copious amounts of research spanning sociological, psychological, and metaphysical fields of study. After meticulously going over years of writing, research, and experiences, I have carefully crafted this cohesive guide for raising little witchlings.

I am not a licensed psychologist, nor am I a professionally trained child-rearing expert. But I am a parent, (at the time of writing this my boys are 6 years old and 6 months old). My elder son was only a few months old when his biological father left, so for almost 5 years I was a solo parent. The one redeeming aspect of 2020 for me and my family is that my partner, Jody, and I got together. He has a 12 year old son, and in September of 2021 Jody and I had a son together. I was proud of being a solo parent, but I was/am honored to now be a stepparent (well, technically, as we aren't married yet), and a co-parent. The transition from one kind of parent to another has been incredible, and if I've learned anything from this experience, it's that, no matter how much help you have, parenting is hard. I know full well that, ultimately, we're just trying to do our best. So, think of this not as a prescriptive guide to parenting, but as a friendly conversation among parents, who may be or are considering becoming, fellow witches or Pagans, who have been down the road you are considering.

I will be frank with you: I am not a perfect parent. I do not have my shit together all the time. I am parent who occasionally cusses, who lets the dishes pile up in the sink, who cries. A parent who will get on the floor and make a total fool of herself just to make her kids laugh. If you want a book written by someone who has perfectly behaved children who say wise things, who feeds their family only organic, locally- or home-grown food, with a beautifully organized house that sits on acres of well-manicured land, then check out my bibliography for a different book. Because you will not find perfection here. Instead, you will find advice, anecdotes, and the accumulation of wisdom gained from years of experience as a witch and a mother, and from writing about being a witch mother in the "Raising Little Witchlings" column for *Witch Way Magazine*, this book has one objective. It is to support you in navigating a path of parenting in which you include your kids in your Craft. Raising a little witchling is not like teaching a student. This process is built upon much more than lesson plans and mentoring. It is an emotional journey of inculturation. Witches have a unique way of viewing the world, of thinking, talking, acting, and relating to each other. It is an investment in the person, and thus the world, you want to nurture. As a witch, magic is likely part of your daily life. As a parent, it will infuse most, if not all, aspects of your childrearing. Conversations about intuiting messages will be as normal as talking about receiving a text or an email. Making plans to look for elves will be as common as going bowling or to see a movie. Witchcraft can be blended seamlessly with ordinary family time because it is a way of life.

WHEN I DECIDED TO RAISE LITTLE WITCHLINGS

I began to consider this journey when my elder child was about a year old. He had just learned to walk and had toddled over to my ancestor altar. He pointed to a photo of my grandmother - who had passed away when I was fourteen - looked up at me with his big, blue eyes, and said, "Gah-mah!" I immediately burst into tears. I cried because I knew he recognized her despite having never met her. It made me question if he had psychic ability. We had never talked about her. And the photo was of my grandmother as a 30-year-old, so my son was not seeing a woman who looked like a grandmother. Most members of my family have naturally strong psychic abilities. I do, as does my mother, grandmother, her mother, and so on, up to my great-great-grandfather, who was the seventh son of a seventh son. So, it came of no surprise that my son had inherited this predisposition for magic.

What did surprise me was how difficult it was to decide if I should raise him as a witch. I knew I did not want my son to struggle the way that I did as a child. Having spiritual gifts can feel isolating and I didn't want him to go through that. I worried that he might be picked on or bullied because he was 'different' as a witchling. I spent months carefully considering this decision. I read anything I could get my hands on and utilized divination and meditation to process and clarify all that I was contemplating. Finally, as we often have to do as parents, after long and thoughtful considering, I decided that this was the path I wanted to take. This path is one that will nurture his spiritual gifts, sate his innate curiosity about and seemingly magnetic attraction towards magic, and would raise him see the world in a way that took me a long time to adopt. I was raised to see anyone different from myself as strange or unusual. Learning witchcraft and adopting paganism shifted my view of the world to one that appreciates the differences between every person on earth. It is one that understands that beauty is not a matter of skin, hair, or body shape, but determined by who someone is on the inside. It's a way of life that encourages empathy, caution, and acting carefully. Finally, my son is, in some ways, so much like me, and in others, he's the total opposite. But even in ways he is different, I know in my heart, my mind, and my spirit that this is the best way to raise him.

Journal Your Journey

I recommend starting a witch parenting journal to record your thoughts, plans, experiences, and expectations. It will serve as diary, baby book, and a written record of your children's journey towards a life of magic and mystery.

TERMINOLOGY

As a Pagan witch, I wrote this with other Pagan witches in mind. However, these techniques may easily be adapted to different spiritualities and magical practices. Witches and Pagans hold many of the same values. So, I am raising my son as both a Pagan and a witch. It just makes sense to incorporate the magical with the spiritual, as the two worlds often overlap. However, 'Pagan' and 'witch' are not interchangeable, so it is important to define what the terms mean to me.

The term Paganism refers to a set of spiritual beliefs that do not adhere to any of the main world religions. A Pagan is "anyone who doesn't follow the teachings of Christianity, Islam, Hinduism, Buddhism, Sikhism, and Judaism," as defined by Tonya Brown in *The Door to Witchcraft*.[1] Paganism is also used as an umbrella term that encompasses earth-based religions, which may be polytheistic or pantheistic, henotheistic, atheistic, or otherwise[2]. According

---

1   Tonya Brown, *The Door to Witchcraft*, (Emeryville: Althea Press, 2019), Chap 1, Kindle.
2   "Paganism," Wikipedia, last modified April 25, 2022, https://en.wikipedia.org/wiki/Paganism

to "What is Paganism?" by Prudence Jones[3], Pagan religions are distinguished by the following qualities:

- Eclecticism

- Respect for plurality

- Belief that views differing from their own are valid

- Venerating nature and the supernatural (that which cannot be defined by science)

- Respect for women and reverence for the Divine Feminine

Jones further argues that Pagans are people who "pursue their own vision of the Divine as a direct and personal experience."[4]

Witchcraft/ Witch

The primary distinction between Paganism and witchcraft is that Paganism is religious and spiritual, while witchcraft entails the manipulation of energy for a specific purpose, or intent. Witchcraft is the work of magic (the release of energy) and psychism (the receipt of energy). It is often practiced by Pagans and often considered an earth-based spirituality. However, not all Pagans practice witchcraft, and not all witches are Pagan. Witches can be of any spirituality or religion, or identify with no religion or spirituality. There are atheist witches, satanic witches, Christian witches – there are witches who keep their spirituality completely separate from their witchcraft, so it doesn't matter what religion or spirituality they are.

In *The Door to Witchcraft*, Tonya Brown argues that witchcraft is, "an empowering practice that any person can learn," explaining that it is "all about stepping outside of our mundane world and choosing to take on a perspective of mysticism and reverence for nature, life, and the energetic forces of this world."[5] Tonya notes that witchcraft, "is about taking the raw, beau-

---

3   Prudence Jones, "What is Paganism?", Pagan Federation International, December 17, 2011, https://www.paganfederation.org/what-is-Paganism/.
4   Prudence Jones, "What is Paganism?"
5   Brown, *The Door to Witchcraft*, Chap 1.

tiful, and powerful forces of our world and using them to create change."[6] For me, witchcraft is about embracing your natural power and utilizing it to find your place in the world and carry out your soul's purpose. It is a way of discovering the flow of life, like matching the rhythm of your breath to that of your child when you hold them and rock them to sleep. Laura Tempest Zakroff quite poetically defines 'witch' in *Weave the Liminal*:

> *"The Witch is the walker between the worlds, the one who resides on the outskirts, the keeper of the mysteries, the righter of ways. The Witch heals, banishes, cleanses, burns, divines, speaks, communes."*[7]

Raven Grimassi posits that one does not learn how to be a witch–either you are or are not a witch. If you determine that you are a witch, then what you learn is "the Arts of Witchcraft…the ways of the Witch."[8] He declares that being a witch "is in your blood, even though it may not be in your lineage".[9] Many witches have been witches in past lives, he explains. Grimassi, like Zakroff, also has a poetic description of the witch:

"The self-styled Witch is a trailblazer…The true Witch was, and is, a subcultural figure. The Witch does not "fit into" the larger social order, but instead makes her or his own way in the background of society. Living between and on the edge, the Witch is the untamed spirit. She or he maintains magic in a world that is burdened with the mundane. For most people, being a Witch is not something one chooses. It is a calling, an inner nature. In the mystical sense, the soul of the Witch returns through reincarnation, experiencing many lifetimes. With each one the Witch reclaims, remembers, and continues to extend the way through the Path of the Witch. It is a sacred quest, moonlit and spirited guided [sic]. In the end, the Witch returns to the stars."[10]

WHO THIS BOOK IS FOR

This book is for parents who want to establish a foundation of spirituality for their family while fostering a sense of individuality and motivating

---

6   Tonya Brown, *The Door to Witchcraft*, chap. 1.
7   Laura Tempest Zakroff, *Weave the Liminal* (Woodbury: Llewellyn Publications, 2019), 2.
8   Grimassi, *What We Knew in the Night*, (Newburyport: Red Wheel/Weiser Book, 2019), 1.
9   Grimassi, *What We Knew in the Night*, 2.
10   Grimassi, *What We Knew in the Night*, 234.

their kids to embrace the magic of life. It is for people who are imperfect, who may or may not have witch parents themselves, or a witch partner, but are passionate about their practice. It is for parents whose spirituality permeates their lives, and who seek to invite their children into their world of magic.

I wrote this book because I want have a conversation with fellow witches that acknowledges the awkward and uncomfortable aspects of parenting, while offering a means to magic that is adaptable to our imperfect, sometimes, impractical, lives. I manifested an incredible, magical life, and I am raising incredible, magical children. Out of gratitude, I want to help other parents find theirs.

BRIEF BREAKDOWN OF THIS BOOK

While there is a Table of Contents listing the title of each chapter, and despite each chapter containing a more detailed overview of subsequent content, I felt a brief breakdown of the book in its' entirety would be helpful. I have broken down the practice of witchcraft into three categories, or aspects: magic, psychism, and earth-based spirituality. The approach I have outlined in this book will help you introduce witchcraft in a way that your children can grow into at their own pace.

Aside from the Introduction and Conclusion, there are seven chapters. The first chapter, "Should I Raise Little Witchlings?", goes over concepts to take into consideration and concerns to address when deciding if this is the best approach for your family. The second chapter, "Embracing and Encouraging Our Children's Emerging Identities", emphasizes the importance of encouraging a child's emerging sense of identity, and offers suggestions for ways to show your children you embrace who they are whole-heartedly. Chapter three, "Welcome to Witchcraft", provides an overview of magic, psychism, and nature-based spirituality, offering ways you can incorporate them into your child's everyday life- i.e. through storytelling, energy work/exercises, mindfulness exercises, etc. This chapter addresses the ethics of magic and how you can determine ethical guidelines you and your family are comfortable with. Chapters 4, 5, and 6 take you through practices and techniques for magic, divination, and nature-based spirituality. I include instructions, directions, and suggestions for spells, rituals, and activities in each "Practices & Techniques" chapter. Chapter 7, "Practicing Parenthood" acknowledges how parenting is something that can only be practiced, but never mastered, serving as a reminder that there is nothing wrong with reaching out for help. I recommend that, as a parent, you should educate yourself whenever you can, however you can, and utilize any and all tools at your disposal. To help you figure out where to go from here I include a list of reading material and resources for you, the parents, as well as your children.

Throughout the book you will find quotes and call-outs. I have chosen the quotes, and designed the call-outs, to keep you mindful, motivated, and, most importantly, to make sure you're taking care of yourself.

Final Thoughts

Raising children amidst the magic of witchcraft is not only an opportunity to introduce them to the magic we've learned, but also for us to learn from the unique magic only children can perceive– creating for them a safe space to share with us their perspective of the world – both seen and unseen. By introducing our children to the art of witchcraft, we provide them an answer to that inner calling towards magic and mystery. They will not have to wonder why they're different, they will not be confused about how they know things they shouldn't – they will know they are naturally adept at magic and predisposed to understanding what their psychic abilities are telling them. Giving them the ability for personal exploration, separate from the mainstream, early in life can be very empowering. Should our children decide that they are not witches, that's okay. They will still be intelligent, considerate, respectful, and wise humans. And who knows, maybe one day they'll realize that they actually do wish to be witches. But in raising our kids as little witchlings, we're laying a path that is well-lit, with firm parameters and forgiving terrain. We're providing our children with skills and tools that will help them confront and overcome anything they'll face in life.

This won't be easy—I don't think anything about parenting is easy, except for loving your children. But it will be enlightening, exciting, and leave you with exquisite memories. If you make a mistake, if you get frustrated, if your children get annoyed and tell you to piss off, don't despair. I forgive you, your children will forgive you. You should forgive yourself. If you find the last bit challenging remember this: you are doing the most complex, challenging, and delicate job in the world, and **you are doing great**.

Chapter 1

SHOULD I RAISE LITTLE WITCHLINGS?

"Above all, watch with glittering eyes the whole world around you,
because the greatest secrets are always hidden in the most unlikely
places. Those who don't believe in magic will never find it."

—ROALD DAHL

WE ALL WANT OUR KIDS TO grow into healthy, responsible, respectable, and respectful adults who are successful in their endeavors and satisfied with who they are. We work to meet our children's physical, emotional, and cognitive needs from the start. Determining how to address our children's spiritual needs can feel daunting. What we teach our kids about morality and belief (either intentionally or not), and the ways in which we shape their perspective, play important roles in creating the person they grow up to be. There are many options and paths we can take that will influence what we teach and how we teach it –this chapter addresses considerations and concerns regarding the path in which children are raised as little witchlings. It would have been much easier for me to commit to this journey if I had a clear idea of these considerations, rather than being left with the sense that I was stepping into a vast unknown, or making things up as I went along. This chapter will open an important conversation about potential challenges on this path, but it will not offer solutions. You know your children better than anyone, and you know what is best for your family. So, I cannot tell you how to overcome these dilemmas. My hope is that in acknowledging these concerns, you are left with a sense of awareness, and thus peace, in your decision. And I want to help you see these questions from different angles and perspectives so that you can choose the right approach for your family. Perhaps by seeing these issues in a new light, you will parent your little witchling with greater confidence, that can lead to greater joy, enhanced creativity, and far less stress and worry.

COMMON CONCERNS

Deciding which concerns to address here was not easy. I wanted to be as inclusive as possible, including those who identify as Pagan, witch, or both, as well as those who may be neither, but are considering these paths for their family. I went through over five years of personal journals, searching for entries in which I confessed uncertainty, worry, or anxiety. I spent countless hours with Google, searching for articles and blogs on witchcraft and parenting, and consumed as many books as I could find on spiritual parenting. I realized that, regardless of what I learn from others, whether they were licensed professionals or experts with a number of degrees, I always go with my instinct. It's reassuring, of course, when the 'experts' on parenting make recommendations that align with my beliefs and/or behaviors, but I noticed I have been, and continue to be, hesitant to change my ways when an 'expert' presents contradictory recommendations. If there is a risk of harming my children in any way, even if it's a slight risk in the distant future, then I would delve into why this 'expert' said what they said, looking for other resources, particularly peer-reviewed studies, that supported their claims. Should there be three or more reputable sources that were in agreement, my next step, depending on the subject matter, would be to consult with my children's pediatrician, or seek advice from friends or relatives. I would perform divination and meditate on the information I received, and only then would I change my approach. These are the concerns this chapter will address:

2

- What is an appropriate age to start learning about witchcraft and Paganism?

- Is it appropriate to do magic with my kids or to let them participate in rituals?

- How can I teach them the importance of authenticity while also encouraging them to keep parts of their spiritual lives private?

What is an appropriate age to start learning about witchcraft and Paganism?

The best time to start tutoring your child about witchcraft and Paganism is when you start instilling in them morals and values. According to Janet Callahan, author of *Parenting Pagan Tots*, "we should start from the beginning. The reasoning is simple: the world is a magical place for children from day one. Giving them a framework to build on and traditions our family follows, gives them a sense of stability, and the ability to call on the Divine no matter how old they are or what problems they face".[11]

The same tools any parent would use to teach their children morality and meaning may be used to introduce your child to earth-based religions, such as movies, stories, folklore, and myths. Experience is the best way to internalize what they learn from a book or a screen. The simplest way to do this is to take your child outside. Introduce them to your favorite tree, to the plants in your garden, or the boulder you like to use for offerings. As you explore, ask your child what they think the tree's name is. Encourage them to talk to the tree, to ask it questions and listen for answers. Visualization is a major part of magic, as well as communing with gods and spirits. Imaginative play will make their visualization skills stronger, so be enthusiastic and emboldening with they pretend play.

Is it appropriate to do magic with my kids or to let them participate in rituals?

Yes! Whether you're working a spell or participating in a ritual, experiencing magic firsthand can be incredibly empowering. Magic shows children that, though they may be small, though they may be young, they have the power to change their lives, and the world around them. Rituals take this

---

11   Janet Callahan, *Parenting Pagan Tots* (self-pub., Kindle, 2015), 101

even further, showing children that they are a part of something greater than themselves. Perhaps it's this great 'other' that has given them their magic, or perhaps they were born with it. That is something your children will determine for themselves, and they are sure to figure that out if they are exposed to magic, especially that of a ritual.

Now, there are of course exceptions – the kind of magic, the ritual setting or intent, may not be appropriate, but that doesn't mean there is no way to safely, comfortably teach them magic, or include them in ritual. Monica Crosson explains in "Under a Blood Moon: A Family Ritual", that including your children in ritual is a "wonderful way to connect spiritually with them, help give them a solid base, foster deep bonds between family members, and provide structure and security"[12]. Start performing rituals at home with your kids, so they can learn what to expect and what to do, should you take them to participate in a group ritual someday. Let them watch you work spells and other forms of magic, too. As their imagination develops, their understanding of the limitations of magic is established, (i.e., that natural laws cannot be broken, no matter how convincing it is on television), and are mature enough so they both understand that what they do- be it magical or not – has the potential to influence the lives of others in unimaginable ways, and that magic worked should be done only after careful consideration, contemplation, and cautious planning. We will get into this more in later chapters, but magic is a neutral force of nature, as ritual is a neutral practice of spirituality. How they are utilized is what matters. If the intention and other particulars of the ritual and/or magic pose no threat to your children's comfort, safety, or well-being, then there is no reason not to include them, at least in an observatory manner.

How can I teach them the importance of authenticity while also encouraging them to keep parts of their spiritual lives private, especially concerning certain people (i.e., Auntie Church-Goer)?

This is a complex dynamic to navigate when raising little witch-lings. While you need to weigh various considerations, such as certain family

12   Monica Crosson, "Under a Blood Moon: A Family Ritual," in *Llewellyn's 2017 Witch's Companion*, ed. Ed Day (Woodbury: Llewellyn Publications, 2016), 166

members who may not understand, or who may react in a way that could be traumatizing to your children, the simplest approach is to come out to all family members so that you do not have to worry about your child 'outing' you. More importantly, you should not burden your child with keeping a secret from friends or family.

However, I know from experience that being open about your spirituality might be more detrimental than keeping it a secret. In my case, my grandmother was a very devout Christian who believed that anyone who does not live according to the Bible is wrong. She would not hesitate to tell my children that they will be banished to hell for their beliefs. I wish this was an exaggeration. I spent much of my life terrified because this is the kind of stuff what she told me when I was growing up. She often talks about her beliefs in front of my son and does respect my request to stop when she says things that I believe are inappropriate for my child to hear. I want my son to know that people are different. And being exposed to other beliefs provides options to explore should he decide that Paganism is not right for him. However, I do not want my grandmother to find out because she would not hesitate to tell my son that he is at risk of being taken by the devil. She would frighten him, tell him scary things about hell and instruct him to go to church. This is not something I want to expose him to.

But how can I do this and avoid asking my son to keep our way of life secret? Secrets, especially those pertaining to significant information, pose a risk of harming my son just as much as having a family member make him feel ashamed, guilty, and burdened with the responsibility of 'saving' my soul, as my grandmother would have it. Dr. Jack Schafer, a behavioral analyst for the FBI, explains in his article, "Why Keeping Secrets Heightens Anxiety and Depression", published May 15, 2021 on PsychologyToday.com, that keeping secrets, "can trigger depression, anxiety, and poor overall personal health," not to mention the stress of, "being on constant guard not to wittingly or unwittingly reveal" the secret.[13] Secrets can also put our kids in physical danger, as predators often use the idea of secrets as a way to hide abuse.

---

13   Jack Schafer, "Why Keeping Secrets Heightens Anxiety and Depression," Psychology Today, May 15, 2021, https://www.psychologytoday.com/us/blog/let-their-words-do-the-talking/202105/why-keeping-secrets-heightens-anxiety-and-depression

We have a "no secrets in our home" policy. We want to establish an environment in which our kids feel comfortable coming to us, trusting that no matter what they divulge, they will not get in trouble. Rather than secrets, we can teach our children about privacy. In addition to keeping their bodies safe, discretion is an important aspect of working magic. We want them to be discrete, determining who they can talk to about their magical workings.

DISCRIMINATION

Discrimination might be a major consideration when contemplating whether to raise your child as a witch or Pagan. While a lot has changed over time, there is still quite a bit of discrimination and prejudice against witches. There is long-steeped historical prejudice against witches; or anyone who is not conforming to the mainstream, which in historical context simply meant anyone going against the Christian church. Movies, television, and other mass media are a product of this, depicting witches as evil, devil-worshiping sadists. Ghost-hunting 'reality' TV shows often claim to find 'demons' and then blame Ouija boards or witchcraft for summoning them.

Admitting to witchcraft or Paganism on the school playground is likely to make your child stand out from the crowd. It would be reasonable to worry about bullying. Discrimination based on race, gender, and sexual orientation is problem in our country. Adding non-traditional spiritual practices to that list could make these challenges even worse, especially for families whose identities intersect in various ways.

Enlightenment Leads to Acceptance

People who reject or judge our way of life often do so because they do not understand what we are about. Like mentioned before, there is such a long history of anyone different from the mainstream being labeled and persecuted, and we still see remnants of that today. Telling someone you reach spirituality differently than they do often causes conflict because their church tells them you're wrong. Not only that, but they've weaved this belief throughout their teachings for hundreds of years. Then they see movies and read books that reinforce this, and they assume that there is truth to it. Sometimes we just have

6

to deal with people who will not accept us. It is a part of life. Prepare your child for this by telling them that they should never let what other people think of them get in the way of being their authentic selves. All they can do is be a kind person and remember that if someone is worth having as a friend, then they will see that, regardless of religious belief.

When my elder son started preschool, I was open with his teacher about our Pagan practices and our belief in magic. I didn't use the word "witch", though. I felt that, while his teacher was eager to learn about Paganism, that she would be put off by the word witch. There are so many negative connotations with the word, and it's not often that you find someone who is willing to hear you out, who wants to learn enough about witches to change their opinion of them. That was the excuse I gave myself, anyways. Now that I look back on it, I realize that I was just scared of pushing my luck. I had not planned to tell his teacher when I first sent him to public school – I couldn't foresee any reason they would need to know. If I kept him home to celebrate a Sabbat, I would simply call and ask the school to excuse his absence as he was staying home for religious observation. The decision to tell his teacher was spur-of-the-moment. She and I were talking about how autumn was a wonderful season and she mentioned wanting to come up with activities for the kids that got them outside and taught them about autumn. I told her how my son and I had made a gratitude tree over the weekend, and, trusting my instincts that it would be well-received, I revealed that it was in celebration of Mabon. To my delight, she was more than simply accepting – she was intrigued. She was really excited, actually. She had heard of Paganism but didn't know what it meant, and thought it was just fantastic to have a student who was Pagan. She asked many questions over the next few days – but a couple minutes during school drop-off and pick-up wasn't ideal for explaining Pagan beliefs and practices. Especially when she wanted my input on how she could teach my son's class about them. As Yule was fast approaching, I offered to write a story book about the holiday. She was thrilled – and inspired to incorporate religions and spiritualities from all around the world in her lesson plans. I would send in gifts or stories or just email his teacher with an activity idea for each of the following Sabbats for the rest of the school year. She loved it. My son loved it too. Now, his teacher and

I agreed from the get go that Josh was not to be singled out. We had no right to share such personal information with his classmates, and I let him know that the decision was his. If he wanted to share with his classmates that he had experience with some of the practices, or shared some of the beliefs, that were addressed in the teacher's lessons about Paganism, then he was absolutely welcome to do that. I told him, if he didn't want to tell the class anything about his beliefs or our family practices, then that is okay too. He is absolutely welcome to keep that to himself. While his classmates never learned that he was Pagan, I am grateful for the experience, and my son is too. It taught us that if people are willing to learn about our way of life, then they are willing to, perhaps even likely to, open their minds and grow to accept us.

CO-PARENTING

As I was used to being a solo parent, it took a while for me to realize that being a mother to my second child would be a completely different experience than it was with my first. I would not be raising my children by myself anymore. This is wonderful, of course, but it was uncharted territory for me. My partner, Jody, and I are quite similar in our approach and our beliefs when it comes to the mundane aspects of parenting, so that made learning to be a co-parent much easier. But it eventually dawned on me that my partner, who is not spiritual at all, much less a Pagan witch, might not be on board with raising our son on my path.

When my second son was an infant, my partner told me that he does not want to raise our kids with any religion or spirituality. He thinks we should allow our children to determine their own beliefs as they grow. I, on the other hand, believe that it is highly beneficial for a child to have a strong spiritual foundation. Therefore, I've been working on establishing a spiritual foundation by raising my elder son as a witch and a Pagan. I encourage nature veneration and the acceptance of magic and realms other than the physical. I emphasize the importance of accepting responsibility for yourself and your actions. My elder son and I do energy work, spells, and lay offerings to nature spirits. I tell him stories of gods and heroes and monsters and faeries.

But I have to take a different approach with my second child. I will raise him in accordance with the same morals and ethics as I do my elder son, but my partner does not want our son to be identified as Pagan unless that is what he chooses to do when he's older.

It is important that we respect not only our co-parents wishes, but our children's, as well. If one child wants to learn about magic and shows enthusiasm about Pagan practices, by all means, continue to teach them. But if they are resistant, seem uncomfortable, or indicate that they do not want to be witches, we should respect that, too. It is not easy having a blended, interfaith family. But we make it work. We communicate, respect each other, and provide a safe space for each person to express their questions, concerns, and suggestions. Even if your co-parent is a Pagan witch, they may have different ideas regarding your children's spirituality, so it is important to communicate with them. If this is the case, it could be beneficial for the family to observe, blend, or create new rituals that fit each persons' spiritual needs and preferences.

Whatever you decide to do, it is important that your children know that you and your co-parent, regardless of beliefs, can work together harmoniously. This teaches your children to be respectful, empathetic, and adaptable, showing them how to work with others, regardless of their differences.

FINAL THOUGHTS

There is a lot to consider when raising a little witchling, but it does not have to be overwhelming. Take your time and approach each question or potential obstacle as if it were the only one you had to face. When you have come to one conclusion, then you can move onto the next. Remember, journaling is a helpful way to work through your worries, hopes, fears, wishes, and feelings about parenting. Raising a family is one of the most difficult things you will do. We are nurturing tiny humans to send out into the world and make it what they will. That is a huge responsibility. But it is one we can accept with confidence and grace. We do not have to be perfect. We just have to love our kids and raise them to the best of our abilities. Are you ready for this adventure? Let's go!

Chapter 2

ENCOURAGING AND EMBRACING OUR CHILDREN'S EMERGING IDENTITIES

"Knowing yourself is the beginning of all wisdom."

—ARISTOTLE

BECOMING A WITCH ENTAILS A TOTAL transformation, requiring the establishment of a new self-awareness. The creation of this witch identity paves the way to other key aspects of a new sense of self. This is true of all witches, no matter their age. However, children may not yet have a complete sense of identity, much less self-awareness. As parents, we help cultivate this in order to prepare them for their initiation into witchcraft.

There are certain skills and behaviors, adopted in a particular order, that can guide a child onto the path of the witch. This process has helped my son become self-aware. Due to cognitive delays and emotional dysregulation, he has had a difficult time finding himself in a social setting. But he is improving. So I know first-hand how powerful the work of identity-building can be.

Laura Tempest Zakroff describes the creation of the witch identity in her book, *Weave the Liminal*. She says that this foundation offers the 'keys to the Witch's path,' which "provide basic guidelines that allow us to tread carefully into deeper territories" [14] Her analogy of three keys is particularly helpful in deciphering the right formula of skills and behaviors that will establish a strong foundation for a witch identity. The three keys to the witch's path are: Know thyself, maintain balance, and accept responsibility. She explains, "these three keys combined can guide you through many situations you will encounter on your path as a Witch...With patience, compassion, and understanding in hand, these keys will empower your path and illuminate your way..."[15] With the three keys in mind, this chapter offers suggestions, anecdotes, and expert opinions regarding children's emerging sense of identity, teaching them empathy, respect, and personal accountability. These concepts are integral aspects of self-awareness, so instilling them early on helps our kids with a number of milestones in the future. Equally important is a child's sense of self in a social setting, which is why the final section of this chapter will provide suggestions on how to foster friendship in a healthy way.

I am going to address each one in the order that proved to be most effective for my son, but that does not mean you must follow my example exactly. The order in which you foster these skills and behaviors will be determined by the receptiveness, age, and the cognitive and psychological capacity of your child.

IDENTITY &
SELF-AWARENESS

Your sense of identity is the understanding of who you are. Children start to develop a sense of identity around eighteen months of age, when they begin to recognize themselves in mirrors, and learn to use words like 'me' and 'mine.' By age two, they have a sense of identity that is based on their social group, typically their family. Their behavior is then motivated by reactions that let them know they are accepted, and that they are performing well in the

---

14   Zakroff, *Weave the Liminal,* 21.
15   Zakroff, *Weave the Liminal,* 22-23.

group.[16] At this time you should be especially mindful of your interactions with your child, and respond to them in a way that reassures their role in the family, encouraging their sense of identity to unfold as they grow. Self-awareness is the first of the three aforementioned "keys to the witch's path". You must know who you are to understand what motivates you, what hinders you, what empowers and emboldens you as well as that which holds the potential to weaken and subdue you. Everyone, and everything, in the universe is intricately connected. Picture a glowing silver strand of spider silk. Normally, a silk strand will connect to another, and the web takes shape as the spider works in an expanding spiral. The web of the universe is like a trippy 3D version of a spider's web. Rather than one strand connecting to another, there are countless strands connecting each life form to other life forms, and no pattern taking form – at least none that our mortal minds can comprehend. Some strands simply connect one life form to the next nearest being, while others span across time and space. This is a mind-boggling concept, right? But it's one that we witches must be mindful of – self-awareness gives us strength to bear the weight of the responsibility of knowing that everything we do will affect another's life. Self-awareness will ensure that we act only when we must, and we only act after we have made sure that what we plan to do will be that which is most likely to manifest our intention with as minimal effect on others as possible.

According to Kids Academy[17], there are particular techniques that will encourage your child's individuality and will have a lasting, positive influence on their development.

- **Help them discover their passion**. Provide them with opportunities to explore different activities, encouraging them to spend time trying those for which they have a fondness.

- **Emphasize the importance of hard work over natural ability**. Something earned and/or learned is more rewarding and sets them up for a solid work ethic later in life.

16   "Childhood and Adolescent Psychology," Lumen Learning, Florida State University at Jacksonville, accessed February 22, 2022, https://courses.lumenlearning.com/atd-fscj-child-psychology/chapter/self-awareness-and-identity-development/.
17   "The Self and Identity: 5 Ways to Encourage Your Child's Individuality". Parent Resources Blog, KidsAcademy.mobi. Last updated January 23, 2017. https://www.kidsacademy.mobi/storytime/self-and-identity-5-ways-encourage-your-childs-individuality/

- **Practice, practice, practice!** When your child has developed a passion for something, establish regular practice sessions doing that activity. It makes them feel good about themselves while giving them the opportunity to improve their skills and abilities.

- **Feel your feels and share them so they heal.** (Yes, I made this up. No, I do not care that it is silly). Encourage your kids to express their feelings and reassure them that their feelings are acceptable. I have to work with my son on how to express his big feelings with a calm body and clear words. Patience is key, folks, *patience is key!*

- **Teach them assertiveness.** According to the "Assertiveness" Wikipedia page, the quality is defined as "being self-assured and confident without being aggressive". We instill this quality by cultivating within our children a sense of pride and teaching them that being different is not a bad thing, but rather something to strive for. Explain to your children and remind them as often as you need to (as patiently as you can), that what sets us apart from others is what makes us who we are. We want them to be proud of who they are and not let others make them feel bad about what they like or do, clothes they wear, beliefs they hold. I often remind my son that everybody is different, and it is the differences that makes people special and worthy of love. I warn him that not everyone understands this. I tell him it is a secret of the wise to love people's differences. He is six- years-old and could not care less about what others think of him. He is not fazed when kids are mean to him about his disabilities or anything else. He lets their words roll off his back like water off a ducks' feathers. When there is an incident at school or at the playground, he will shrug and say, "I like myself. I think it's sad that 'so-and-so' isn't grateful for the things that make people different." Even though I have heard him say this at least a dozen times, I cannot help but swell with pride. I have never put it into those terms, but in his sweet, complicated mind, that is how my words have translated: to accept another's differences is to be grateful for what makes them special.

- **Let them fall, fail, and get frustrated.** It is natural to want to protect your child. I know it just as well as the next. My partner and I often joke that we take 'helicopter parenting' to the next level because we hover around our baby, making sure he does not bonk himself in the head or poke himself in the eye. But letting kids fail teaches them how to turn failure into success. It teaches them to think outside the box, how to be a little more careful, a little more aware of themselves and their surroundings, and teaches them how to consider what they did wrong and how to do things differently next time.

Encouraging your child to be who they truly are will serve them well, especially as witches-in-training. Witches should be, or at least strive to be, self-aware. Self-awareness refers to the ability to know yourself in an objective manner, without your ego or emotions misconstruing your perception of yourself. A person could easily convince themself that they are excellent at time management, for example, but in reality, they are often late. Let's say this hypothetical person is referred to as "Always Late Lenny" because they are so rarely on time for things. Lenny does not want to admit that they have an incorrect perception of themself, though. Why they can't is something Lenny must figure out for themselves. Until they do, whenever they contradict an idea they have about themselves, they are going to place the blame elsewhere. If someone or something else was the reason they were late, then it isn't their fault – they can still believe they are efficient with time management.

That meme of "how I think I look- how others think I look- how I actually look" comes to mind. To be self-aware means that all three boxes depict the same image. According to Meredith Betz (2021), this is a rare skill, but an important one in terms of success in adulthood. It is important for witches because we manipulate the world around us. So we must be very aware of what we do so that we do not inadvertently harm anyone. We have to understand why we want what we want, as this will help us differentiate between a desperate need and a reactive whim.

TEACHING
EMPATHY & RESPECT

Empathy is the ability to understand a situation from the viewpoint of another person, enabling you to anticipate how they feel. This allows you to understand people on a deeper level, especially when it comes to understanding why they do what they do. I believe that empathy and respect go hand in hand - when we learn how to empathize, we develop respect for a person. Thomas Lickona, Ph.D., a developmental psychologist, defines respect as, "showing regard for the intrinsic worth of someone."[18] (Newman, 2021). If we teach our kids that everyone is worthy of respect, and encourage them to empathize, then behaving in a respectful manner will come much easier - especially in relation to person who is not respectful towards them. Our kids may face disrespect for their beliefs, and the sooner we teach them to behave respectfully to everyone, no matter how they are treated, the more ingrained it will be in their personality by the time they face such adversity.

Showing Self-Care, Supporting Self-Love

We teach our children by example more than we could ever know. That is why it is important for you and for them to practice self-care. Self-care leads to self-love, which is one of our main objectives as parents.

The best way to teach empathy is to encourage your child to put themselves in another's situation, reminding them that other people have feelings, just as they do. Telling your kids about situations you deal with, particularly how they made you feel and how you reacted to those feelings, gives them an idea of how others experience emotions. But it also offers ways of handling 'big feelings.' They need to know that 'big feelings' are always big, they do not shrink because your body gets bigger. If anything, they get even bigger, so the sooner you learn how to manage those feelings with healthy coping mechanisms, the better.

Teaching respect will go a long way in teaching empathy. The simplest way to teach respect is to lead by example: be respectful to your children, and clearly outline how they are expected to behave towards you (i.e., respectfully), they will learn how to be respectful towards others.

---

18   Catherine Newman, "10 Simple Ways to Raise a Respectful Child," *Parents*, last modified March 19, 2021, https://www.parents.com/parenting/better-parenting/positive/how-to-raise-a-respectful-child/

Catherine Newman, of *Parents* magazine, outlines ways to teach respect. Simple things, such as allowing your child to choose between two outfits, teaches the child that they are valued. This shows respect for who they are as an individual and reinforces their need to feel accepted. An example Newman uses is is to let your child wear mismatched socks. Giving your children your full attention and speaking politely, using manners, and supporting their opinions, are great ways to teach by example. Even if you do not agree with their opinion, it is important to commend them for their input, and explain why you will not be going with their suggestion. Newman also suggests teaching children about other cultures and ways of life, to "cultivate curiosity," showing them the beauty of people in how different they can be from one another.[19] (10 Simple Ways to Raise a Respectful Child, 2021). There is a quote by Annie Gottlieb that I absolutely love and is one that perfectly depicts the way my son understands respect: "*Respect is appreciation of the separateness of the other person, of the ways in which he or she is unique.*"

The sooner we start working to instill these skills -respect, personal accountability, independence, self-respect and self-confidence – the better. They will think, act, and behave as witches do – carefully, with consideration and a healthy amount of caution. There are some of you reading this that may learn that your children don't want to be witches – and if they don't, that's okay. At least we have established in them a skill set that will put them on a path of gratitude, empathy, respect... the path of love. And speaking of love, children need a lot of it. More than we could give them – and we give them an incredible amount! But regardless, they still need more, so let's address our children's social lives.

SETTING THE SOCIAL SCENE

As adults our social lives often take the back burner, focusing on work and family first (not necessarily in that order – sometimes putting work first *is* putting your family first). But kids need social lives. It is vital to their development, helping to shape who they are and who they will grow up to be. According to Dr. Vincent Iannelli, of Very Well Family's

19   Newman, "10 Simple Ways to Raise a Respectful Child"

parental advice page, a healthy friendship can play an integral role in a child's emotional development, helping with the establishment of effective communication skills, emotional regulation, and learning how to constructively express themselves.[20] Social interaction is particularly relevant for little witchlings because interacting with other little witchlings can help to establish the social norms of our subculture. Socializing with other little witchlings will either reinforce that which we are teaching them, or will provide the opportunity to learn different beliefs about magic and see alternative views about life and the Divine- either way, it will be beneficial for our kids. The occult community is knit closer together with every friendship forged. Laura Tempest Zakroff puts it quite beautifully in "A Witch's Guide to Essential Etiquette" (2018), saying, "Value everyone you come across and treat them with respect, whether you know who they are or not. Often, amazing power can come from the most unassuming of packages, especially if given a change to thrive. Community is built by recognizing the importance of all..."[21]

Kids socialize at school, but their peer interactions are limited – they are able to roam about the yard with their pals for a 15 minutes or so before recess ends and they must return to learning. They may get to interact socially during certain classes – such as Physical Education, or during group projects in Science or English class. But we want to provide our children the opportunity to befriend a variety of people, both magical and mundane, and, if possible, in an environment that encourages the (respectful) exchange of ideas, beliefs, and practices.

Whether you're a witch parent or not, it's important to make sure your children have the opportunity to socialize with other kids. As witch parents, we want to socialize our kids with other little witchlings- as well as with kids from non-magical families. Let's start with other little witchlings. Where do we start? Those who practice with a group of witches, whether you are in a coven, or belong to a temple or tradition, have already overcome

20   Iannelli, Vincent, "How Kids Make and Keep Friends," VeryWellFamily, last updated July 21, 2021, https://www.verywellfamily.com/making-and-keeping-friends-2633627#toc-why-friendships-are-important
21   Laura Tempest Zakroff, "A Witch's Guide to Essential Etiquette", from *Llewellyn's 2019 Witches' Companion*, ed. Andrea Neff (Woodbury, MN: Llewellyn Publications, 2018), 41.

the biggest hurdle - which is finding other witches. If your meetings are strictly "No Kid Zones," you could propose to the group that you designate certain meetings as kid friendly, and then work with them to prepare rituals and activities that would be appealing and beneficial for kids of all ages.

While being a solitary witch is wonderful, it can be a bit alienating. I want my kid to meet other witch kids, but I do not want to join a coven to make that happen, either. That is why, instead of trying to put together a Pagan youth group, or coordinate kid-friendly magical events, I could establish a group that welcomes families of any belief system. This plan comes with downfalls, of course. It would take a lot of time and a lot of work. I mean, for me personally, I live in an area that's predominantly Christian. The group would have to be planned very carefully, paying meticulous attention to activities and language that would be as inclusive as possible.

The thing is, however, I'm shy. Super shy. So as wonderful as an idea as that is for you outgoing, adventurous folk, it wouldn't be ideal for me. I'd be more inclined to look for an event, festival, even a camp program for Pagan families (or at least for little witchlings). A search on Google will help you locate events near your home. The Pagan Pride Project is one event that takes place in most states, and so the chances are pretty good that you will find one that is within driving distance. Retreats, camps, and the like, are really helpful because the offer the space to create deeper connections. A great youth group is Spiral Scouts, which is like the Boy Scouts, but for Pagan kids. The only potential downfall to this option is that the charters are few and far between. However, you can go to their web page if you wish to start a charter near you.

Should there be limited options for in-person events, there's always online events for families. This route would most likely be geared for families of a specific ideology – Pagan, Christian, Islam, etc. And that's okay. Even if you can only find online events for little witchlings, or Pagan families, it's still a great place to start. It's rare to find two Pagan or witch families who have the same beliefs, the same practices, the same methods – and the idea is to find friends for our little witchlings that have some things in common, and a lot to teach each other.

FINAL THOUGHTS

The key takeaway for this chapter is to lead by example. If we are supportive, encouraging, empathetic, and open with our children, they will grow up to be the same way. It may require patience, we just have to take a breath, count to ten, fix a smile on our face, and practice our mindfulness training. If you need to take a break, take one. If you need to go outside to scream, do it. We are parents and we are witches. So we've got this.

Chapter 3

WELCOME TO WITCHCRAFT!

"Knowing you are a Witch is a matter of inner discovery. It's recognition and it's acknowledgment...Being a Witch is in your blood, even though it may not be in your lineage."

—RAVEN GRIMASSI

YOU FEEL CONFIDENT, AND HOPEFULLY EXCITED, to lay a foundation of practices that will shape your child into a kind, respectful, responsible adult who will be able to enhance their life with magic. Raising our children as witches will provide them with the wisdom and tools they will need in order to pursue their own vision of the Divine. They will learn to respect and utilize the energy and spirit of the soil, plants, rocks, trees, and everything else they fall in love with. We provide for them a stable environment that is encouraging and supportive, and that also prepares them for the real world.

You are taking an approach to parenting that encourages kids to be themselves, to be confident and assertive, while also being respectful, considerate, and appreciative of all peoples and ways of life. But there is more to being a witch than these things. Our path is greater than working spells and reading Tarot.

Witchcraft is an art, a practice, and a way of life. Witches are mindful creatures who are grateful for what they have and for who they are. We have a firm sense of ethics by which we must abide. We use magic responsibly. We work to connect with the seen and unseen worlds. It is this basic makeup of a witch that we are going to work towards establishing in this chapter, effectively preparing our kids for working with magic, practicing divination, and delving into a spirituality that calls out to them. Children are born with an awareness of the beings of the unseen world, so it is not a matter of convincing them of what or who is out there. As Raven Grimassi states in *What We Knew in the Night* (2019), witchcraft is "a sentient spirit...It resides within you and passes out through you into the world...Knowing you are a Witch is a matter of inner discovery."[22] It is about teaching them how to safely explore the unseen world, while using their powers responsibly. To prepare them for this, we are going to work on building skills that will help them with visualization, mindfulness, and manifesting their will.

BENEFITS OF STORYTELLING

Humans have been telling stories since the beginning. According to anthropology, images on cave walls were not done to display one's artistic abilities, but to serve as visual aids for storytelling. The practice of storytelling has existed so long in human history that our brains have adapted to the practice, evolving so that we learn through storytelling. It is clear that this magical practice offers benefits beyond entertainment or education, though, particularly for children. Storytelling has an absolutely magical effect on them.

Storytelling has an inherent magic that is experienced by people listening to it. But if the person telling the story understands magic, the teller can utilize that magic and direct it to manifest their will, thereby actively experiencing the magic as well. The audience aids in the magical working, as energy is raised by their imagining and empathizing with the people and places of the story.

22   Raven Grimassi, *What We Knew in the Night*, (Newburyport, MA: Red Wheel/Weiser Books, 2019), 1.

The magic of storytelling comes from the most basic component of the practice: the spoken word. Lisa Marie Basile, in her book, *The Magical Writing Grimoire*, explains that "the word itself builds worlds, casts a spell, sets a thing into motion. The word is at the center of all creation and plays a sacred role in many cultures. The word "spell" itself, which is defined as "to tell" or "an utterance," became associated with magic in the Middle Ages, as if to speak something is to cause tangible change."[23]

So, by speaking the words, you and your audience are then able to visualize the scenes, imagine the sounds, smells, textures, and tastes. You will keep your goal in mind, seeing it met when the characters in the story meet theirs. You will see your desires obtained as the characters in the story obtain theirs. The story may speak to your situation metaphorically, or it may be a personal anecdote of what you wish to happen, told as though it already has. The wonderful thing about this is that the spell will use energy from not only yourself but the audience as well. Their thoughts and their feelings only add to the manifestation of your will. And it is so easy a child can do it. Our children can do it.

Your kids should be familiar with the concept of stories and that they have a beginning, middle, and end; plot and characters; action and so on. A story-spell is still a story, after all. Kids of any age can do this, as long as they have developed basic language skills. My son has a speech delay, but it still works for him for two reasons: he knows what he is saying, and he sees it happening in his mind. Kids love the creative freedom they have over this form of magic, too. They can make up characters who are really themselves in "imagination" form, as my son and I have termed it, or they can tell the story using themselves as the main protagonist.

Working the Story-Spell

Once, my son and I went to Chicago for vacation. We stayed with one of my closest friends. She has three kids, and her middle child is my son's age. They hit it off immediately. My son missed him the moment we left, and every few days after we got home, my son would tell me he misses his friend. I taught him to work spells through storytelling, so the first spell he chose

23   Lisa Marie Basile, 2020 pg 14

was to be able to play with his friend. I already had plans to visit again. So I thought that my son would gain confidence that his spell worked, since he would, in fact, play with his friend soon.

He and I worked out the story over the span of two weeks, he told this story repeatedly. We added to it, bringing more details and life to the tale. About three weeks later, my friend texted to tell me she was coming to visit family and asked if she could stay with us. I was floored. I did not think we would see them for several months!

GROWING UP GRATEFUL

As witches, we know the importance of gratitude. We understand that without it, we are all but powerless. So why do we teach our children to say, "thank you," and leave it at that? Gratitude empowers so much of our work as witches. We should establish that foundation as we raise our kids, rather than let them figure it out for themselves as adults. Gratitude is especially important for our little witchlings because without gratitude we cannot manifest, and if we cannot manifest, magic loses its spark.

This goes way beyond being thankful in the moment when you receive something or when someone does something for you. Gratitude is a deep emotion that seems to flow through your entire being when you are flooded with appreciation for something you love. Gratitude is not just something you do or feel: it is a way of life. Every day that you are mindful of what you have, you feel grateful from the bottom of your soul.

Gratitude is a powerful force. It has the ability to manifest wealth, success, healthy relationships. Even non-magical people use this force to manifest their desires (vision boards, journaling, and self-help). It brings not only happiness, which can be fleeting, but *contentment*. To be content is to be satisfied. And to be satisfied is to have a constant level of happiness that can be built upon.

Gratitude reduces stress while simultaneously equipping a person with the ability to cope with trauma and stress in a healthy manner. Studies have shown that those who consciously express gratitude are less likely to suffer from depression, anxiety, and other psychological issues, as well as physical ailments like high blood pressure or obesity. Children who practice gratitude have healthier, more meaningful relationships and have been found to have a stronger moral code. Layous and Lyubomirsky (2014) assert that gratitude has a moral effect, in that it helps kids recognize good deeds in others. Not only are they motivated to reciprocate, but they become more likely to pay it forward, as well.

Summer Allen, writing for the Greater Good Science Center of UC Berkeley, calls gratitude the "mother of all virtues," because it encourages the development of other virtues, *"given its role as 'social glue,' it should not be surprising that evidence points to gratitude's social benefits as well. Research suggests that gratitude inspires people to be more generous, kind, and helpful (or 'prosocial'); strengthens relationships, including romantic relationships; and may improve the climate in workplaces."*[24]

What I found particularly important about correlations between gratitude and children is that there are studies that suggest, "gratitude may play a role in developing purpose"[25] As witches, our sense of purpose is our vocation, identity, and craft. As our children continue down their own paths, they will have a sense of purpose unique to their Craft. What makes me feel all warm and fuzzy is that, by fostering gratitude in my son now, he will have a sense of purpose before he stumbles into his own witchcraft.

I have included some recommendations for activities that will introduce your child to gratitude. Some are better suited to older kids, while others are best for little ones under the age of four. I did not organize the activities into age groups, however, because one's age is not always indicative of developmental level. So, I have simply listed them, starting with activities I am doing with my son now, and ending with ones I plan to do when he is a teenager.

- **"I love _____ because..."** Each day we take a moment to choose something, usually a toy, but sometimes it is the house, furniture, or a person, and talk about why we love it and why it is special. My son will then wrap up our practice by saying, "I love you [object/place/thing/person], thank you for

---

24   Summer Allen, *The Science of Gratitude*, (Greater Good Science Center of UC Berkeley, May 2018) 5, https://ggsc.berkeley.edu/images/uploads/GGSC-JTF_White_Paper-Gratitude-FINAL.pdf
25   Allen, *The Science of Gratitude*, 39

being mine!" He came up with this practice! I had been asking him, "how'd you get this? What do you like about it?" After a few months, feelings of gratitude have started to bud in his little soul.

- **"They're so nice!"** We play this game when we go on walks or are waiting for an appointment. We pick one person in our life and simply talk about why they are nice or why we love them. This activity not only generates appreciation for people, but it is a great way to practice mindfulness with a child.

- **Start a thank you collage, jar, or book.** Writing in journals is a great activity for older kids. For children with short attention spans, or who have difficulty reading or writing, modifying gratitude journaling into a craft will have the same results. Decorate a jar, and each day, write down or draw a picture of something for which you are thankful. Or get a scrapbook and dedicate pages to things for which you are grateful.

- **Host a gratitude awards ceremony.** At the end of the month, pull the gratitude entries from the jar and tally them up. The kids can make awards, and the family can vote on who will represent the top choices. Decorate a designated space, dress in your finest, and pick a host to announce the runner up and the winner. Keep track of the winners throughout the year. Then annually, for instance, at Mabon, hold a ceremony to pick the champion. Make rewards together, and the competitiveness and fuss over the activity will surely draw the interest of kids of any age.

- **Start a (handmade) gratitude journal.** Let your child pick out a special notebook or journal and encourage them to write in it every day. You can even make a journal with your child by combining paper collected from half-full notebooks that are laying around. This is something you and your kid(s) can do together, each having a hand in the decoration and style. The first entry could be expressing appreciation for crafts, for quality time together, or for recycling half-used notebooks. If your child is either too young or not ready to keep a notebook of their own, you could share your entries with them.

- **Design your own practice.** This is more applicable to teens who want to assert their independence. Their gratitude practice may change quite a bit at this time, and you will have to step back and let them take the lead. Encourage them to design their own practice, or even make suggestions for the whole family. That will show them that you respect their ideas and have confidence in their intelligence. It also gives them the freedom they need to develop a sense of self.

While individual practices will vary, fostering gratitude in a child will entail the same components for everyone: consistency, determination, and a sense of humor. Patience has proven to be an invaluable virtue in my case. Kids thrive from consistency, and you must be determined not only to advise, but model the behavior. Of all of these qualities, however, a sense of humor is the most important. This is what is going to keep the activities interesting, beneficial, and, moreover, something your kids *want* to do. If you are overly serious and turn the practice into a somber affair, then it will just feel like a chore.

While gratitude is something that should be practiced year-round, there is particular emphasis on it in the fall. That was the season in which many of our ancestors harvested and stored the food that kept them alive through the winter. It is a way to start the dark season on a light note. This would make a great time to get your kids into the habit of being grateful, and what better way to teach them than with a game?

The Gratitude Game

This game is simple. Sit down with your family and come up with a point system for different activities. For example:

- Make a gratitude jar: 30 points

- Make a gratitude journal: 30 points

- Write and send a thank you letter: 30 points

- Write a thank you card: 20 points

- Write an entry in a gratitude journal: 10 points

- Put an entry into gratitude jar: 5 points

- Recount your favorite part of the day over supper: 5 points

- Come up with ideas for prizes. Whoever earns the most points at the end of the month wins! Keep the game going each month. It takes twenty-one days to form a new habit, so by the end of the first month, your kids will already be viewing the world from a more appreciative standpoint.

Gratitude Quotes

You can bolster your little witchlings' attitude of gratitude by hanging quotes around the house. I have included a few of my favorites:

- *"When I started counting my blessings, my whole life turned around."*
  —Willie Nelson

- *"As we express our gratitude, we must never forget that the highest appreciation is not to utter words, but to live by them."*
  —President John F. Kennedy

- *"Always have an attitude of gratitude."*
  —Sterling K. Brown

- *"Be thankful for what you have; you'll end up having more. If you concentrate on what you don't have, you will never have enough."* —Oprah Winfrey

- *"Unless someone like you cares a whole awful lot, nothing is going to get better. It's not."*
  —Dr. Seuss

- *"You have no cause for anything but gratitude and joy."*
  —Buddha

Seeing quotes and positive affirmations daily can help kids get into the habit of practicing gratitude, because seeing them – either on a conscious or subconscious level. While helpful, passive approaches to gratitude, i.e., Posters of quote, may not be exciting to kids, and if they are, it's not likely to last long. But those posters will still have an effect on them. This is why I think taking an active and passive approach to gratitude will have the strongest impact. The active approaches will help kids experience gratitude, while passive approaches will teach them definitions, highlight benefits, and explore ways other people practice, or feel, about gratitude.

Bedtime is a great opportunity to spend a few minutes on a gratitude activity. People, including children, often wrestle with stressful thoughts when they go to bed. Focusing on gratitude pushes these nagging thoughts to the back of our minds, freeing us from the stress that acts as a guard dog, scaring off sleep whenever it comes too close. A lovely activity is a nightly ritual of reciting things to be thankful for, writing/reciting poems about gratitude, or sharing a story about an event or incident for which they are grateful.

Try writing or collecting gratitude prayers, as they can be recited just before sleep on nights that you and your kids either do not have the time or energy to do a larger activity. I use the term 'prayer' instead of quote or poem, because the short verses are said with intention, which is the defining factor of prayer. While I think you and your family should either write or look for gratitude prayers on your own, curating a collection that resonates with your kid, I will share a prayer I wrote to get you started. It was inspired by the book, *Goodnight Moon*.

Thank you Far,
Thank you, Near

Thank you, Moon, thank you, Stars,
Thank you, Aliens, who might be on Mars.
Thank you, Feet, thank you, Head,
Thank you, Body, that's warm in bed.

Thank you, Far, Thank you, Near,
Thank you, for the Life I hold dear.

Thank you, Sky, thank you, Sun,
Thank you, Day, and your promise of fun.
Thank you, Heart, thank you, Mind,
Thank you, Adventure, for always being easy to find.

Thank you, Far, Thank you, Near,
Thank you, for the Life I hold dear.

Thank you, Magic, thank you, Power,
Thank you, Mind, and the knowledge you devour.
Thank you, Family, thank you, Friend,
Thank you, Love, because you never end.

Thank you, Far, Thank you, Near,
Thank you, for the Life I hold dear.

The intention of this prayer is two-fold. The first is to foster gratitude in your child's life. The second is to help the child see that there are always things for which to be grateful. You are welcome to use this prayer with your children, leaving it as it is, or making any changes you or your child think it needs.

I am sure you and your little witchlings will enjoy making gratitude posters, jars, journals, and cards. I know my son and I do! It is a great way to teach our kids to be good people and to teach them about appreciation. I could honestly go on all day about the benefits of being mindful of gratitude, but this is definitely something you will see for yourself.

Spirits of Place

Taking care of your home physically is a great way to start practicing gratitude. But, unless we include the spirit of the home, or the house spirit, we are not addressing all of our home's needs. Working with the spirit of your home is an excellent way to introduce your kids to spirit work. Fae, deities, and the like, are often overwhelming, even for experienced adult witches, so start with gentle spirits. House spirits are not all sunshine and rainbows, of course—they really do not like filth or disorder, and disgruntled house spirits have been known to cause problems. However, as long as you are showing your home care on a regular basis, you should not have anything to worry about.

As with most beings of the unseen world, a great way to start a relationship with a house spirit is to build an altar for it. The altar can be as elaborate or as simple as you would like. Create a routine of going before the altar with your little witchlings to thank the house, giving it an offering- milk and sweets are common choices - and take a few moments to communicate with it. Acknowledge that the house spirit was there first and will continue to be there after you, and let it know you are grateful that it is sharing the space.

Show your respect and admiration by trying to learn more about the spirit: find out if it has a name it would like to be called, if it is happy, and if there is anything it would like you to do for it. If you are having a spot of bad luck, ask for its blessing. If you have a stain on the rug that will not come out, or a faucet with a leak that cannot seem to be fixed, ask for a little assistance. The house spirit may be happy to lend a hand in exchange for a portion of the family supper, a dish of fresh milk, or a dollop of cream.

Working with the house spirit will not only introduce your little witchlings to spirit work, but it will help instill in them a sense of tradition, lay the foundation for a spiritual practice, and strengthen their psychic abilities. If your kids take easily to communicating and working with the house spirit, you can help them expand their magical allies by introducing them to spirits of plant life growing outside or of potted plants inside.

When your kids learn to work with a variety of spirits, they will quickly discern the difference between them, which is a sign that they may be ready to move on to more powerful spirits. As always, be mindful of your children's reactions and feelings toward the work. If they are frightened or worried, let them know that it is perfectly natural to feel that way and, as a family, work out ways to address their unease.

FINAL THOUGHTS

There is a lot to being a witch, but we are going to make the transition easy as possible for the little witchlings. With activities that are fun and interesting, and particularly geared towards our kids' interests, we lay the foundations of witchcraft subtly and with style.

One thing we must keep in mind is that a witchcraft practice is as unique as the practitioner, so we must be open to our children's unique way of doing things. If they need to visualize by focusing on sounds they hear, or scents they smell, then encourage this. If they want to keep rocks they find in their sock drawer, let them. If they feel that soda can tabs have special powers, by all means, respond with enthusiasm and excitement when they collect a jar full of them. It may feel like pretending, but if you remind yourself that every interaction with your child influences the witch they will become, it enables you to feel more genuine.

The next three chapters will require a lot of patience on your part, as we are going to dive into practices and techniques for magic, divination, and earth-based spirituality. The time we have spent preparing our children will be put to the test when we introduce these practices, as they build on the foundation you've created for them. But you are a witch, so I am confident that you will do an amazing job.

Chapter 4

PRACTICES & TECHNIQUES: MAGIC

"...We are all powerful, beautiful, and capable of changing the world with our bare hands."

—DIANNE SYLVAN, *THE BODY SACRED*

MAGIC IS A COMPLEX, YET INCREDIBLY simple, concept. It is easy to work, but challenging to understand. So we have a lot of ground to cover. Magic is the manipulation of energy in order to create change. As we well know, we are connected to the world around us and all who inhabit it. When we make changes in our lives, we affect everything around us. That is a big deal. So I am going to start this chapter by addressing the ethics of magic and how to establish an ethical code for your family. From there we will move on to the basics of energy work, as magic entails the understanding and manipulation of energy. Following this we will discuss using tools to direct energy. Then we will explore the elements. Finally, we will explore some basic magic that your kids can try.

ETHICS OF MAGIC

Witches tend to create systems that help them make the wisest decisions. Your values and ethics comprise the foundation upon which our practices are built. When a witch belongs to a tradition or church, they have rules and regulations to which they must adhere, and leaders to tell them how to practice. Solitary and eclectic witches have no one telling us what to do. This can be a blessing, but often leaves us feeling lost or confused. How do we find a path that will lead us to our most-desired destination in life? We establish our values, design our ethical guidelines, and weave witchcraft into everything we do all on our own. By so doing, you can perceive the cause and effect of your involvement and in turn, create more mindfulness of your actions.

Ethics are an integral part of witchcraft because witches deal with magics that could have profound implications. Ethical guidelines help us to make wise, effective, efficient decisions. Ethics keep us authentic. We devise ethical guidelines by following our moral code, the shining star that is our personal guidance system. We must be realistic about our strengths and capabilities, and honest about our weaknesses and struggles.

In the context of witchcraft, a witch's ethical code is a set of rules defining what is "good" and what is "bad." If you belong to a tradition, church, or sect of some kind, chances are they have a set of rules outlining ethical behaviors.

But what if you are a solitary, eclectic witch?
How do you create a magical moral code?

As a witch, you should feel empowered to follow your own internal compass. One definition Laura Zakroff offers for the word "witch" is, "one who bends or changes."[26] You should consider your ethical guidelines malleable and revisit them to make sure they are appropriate for where you are in your path. Witchcraft is a living, breathing entity, always growing and always changing. Integral parts of your practice must adjust and grow along with the rest of you, or it will stagnate.

I devised a process called, "The Three Cs of Ethics,": compare, consult, and contemplate. I compare the ethical codes of other witches, covens,

---

26   Zakroff, *Weave the Liminal*, 94.

traditions, and churches, to see what they entailed – to see what aspects of life were most important to them, and to give myself an idea as to where to start. After comparing and contemplating what I have learned, I consult with friends, family, mentors, or acquaintances. Consulting with other witches is helpful because they could offer a perspective you had not considered. Consulting with others helps to reaffirm how I feel about certain things. It may provide me with a perspective on a topic I hadn't considered, too, changing my mind on the subject. I do not consult because I want others approval, or because I am insecure. I want to make sure that I have considered each component thoroughly, and consulting with others is a great way to uncover that which you overlooked.

The aforementioned "compare" phase of devising my own set of ethical guidelines, entailed the examination of several sets of codes, laws, rules, and guidelines of various magical traditions, groups, and individual witches. I found that there were commonalities in each set of ethics. These overarching themes were spells for personal gain, performing magic for others, and magical retaliation, the latter which involves the Rule of Three. Spells for personal gain are spells worked to manifest an intention that benefits the practitioner, i.e., spells to attract wealth, success, victory, etc. These spells offer no benefit to others – except, perhaps the practitioners family. Performing magic for others is fairly self explanatory, determining whether it's ethical to work magic on the behalf of another person and circumstances that would influence the ethical standing of this act. Magical retaliation is magic performed, either in the form of spells or rituals, as a reaction to the actions of others, for the purpose of serving justice, getting revenge, or protection of oneself or others.

Spells for Personal Gain

Many ethical codes prohibit the use of spells for personal gain. The reasons for the prohibition vary – some may feel that it puts non-magical folks at a disadvantage, while others feel it's irresponsible because magic should be used to benefit the greater good. I could go on, but I think it's important for you and your family to contemplate the purpose of working spells and decide for yourselves whether you feel that intentions that fall under personal gain are ethical. Personally, I am of the belief that we cannot help others until we help ourselves. However, if there is any chance that my spell could have a direct influence on another person – such as, causing someone to unjustly lose their job so I can be hired, then I am very careful about how I work the spell. I believe it's perfectly acceptable to work spells of personal gain, so long as they are not at the expense of others.

Performing Magic for Others

The performance of magic for others was, more often than not, allowed only under the condition of informed consent. In some instances, there was an addendum expressing the prohibition of magic for non-magical folks, who were presumed to be unversed in the ways of witchcraft and, therefore, unable to provide informed consent. There have been witches I've communicated with via social media who feel that it's only ethical to work magic for another if the person made the request for a spell on their own volition, feeling that offering to perform magic could influence the third party's decision. I'm not sure how the offer of a spell could be an imposition on the will of the third party -perhaps they aren't sure of what they want but liked the way you phrased the intention, so they agreed without thinking about what the intent is asking for specifically? Or maybe they felt intimidated by your offer, due to feelings of confusion, ignorance, or even fear of magic? I'm sure those witches had very good reasons for feeling this way, I'm just not sure what they are. There were other witches whose ethical code went the other direction, deeming spells for others as ethical, and dismissing the prerequisite of obtaining informed consent if the practitioner had only the best intentions – so, if it's for the persons' own good, they don't have to give consent for the magic to be worked on their behalf.

I feel comfortable working magic for others in general. There are always situations where I may refuse, i.e., if a friend asks me to cast a curse on their ex-boyfriend causing him to get hurt or lose his job, if someone wants me to use glamour magic on them to help them get a job by making their potential employer believe they have qualities they actually lack. I also refrain from offering to perform magic for people who I know to be skeptical/do not believe in, uncomfortable with, or weary of witchcraft. I think it would just be an awkward situation, offering to work a spell to, say ensure safe travels on vacation just to have the person either decline, pointing out that they don't believe in magic, or accept because they think it's the polite thing to do, but in reality they don't believe it would work. That pessimism, even if it isn't outwardly expressed, will actively work against my magic. In short- it would be a waste of my time. My code is what's right for me, though. You and your family have to decide what 's right for you.

Magical Retaliation

Ethical standpoints regarding magical retaliation range from 'harm none' to baneful cursing. Magical retaliation, at its core, involves issues of harm and free will. When you are evaluating ethical guidelines for magical retaliation, you must take into consideration the level of harm and the extent of imposition on free will that you deem appropriate for the situation. For example, determining whether it's acceptable to banish someone who is abusive and toxic -you'd do it to protect yourself from their abuse, and would not cause them any harm, but it would, however, be an imposition on their free will.

Another concept related to the theme of magical retaliation is fear of the consequences for the spell you have worked, particularly by those who ascribe to the Three-Fold Law (whatever you put out into the world will come back to you threefold). Even if you do not ascribe to this belief, however, there are always consequences to our actions. So you have to be sure that serving justice will be worth it – whether 'it' is getting a taste of your own medicine or something more, unexpected and unforeseen.

Wicca is a religion of Witchcraft that relies on tradition and lineage. As a religion, it has set guidelines for its members. One is the law of "Harm None," known as the Wiccan Rede. Many witches, Wiccan and non-Wiccan, abide by this rule, and it is often considered as a basis for the ethical guidelines of magic.

> *Bide the Wiccan Law ye must,*
> *In perfect love and perfect trust.*
> *Eight words the Wiccan Rede fulfill:*
> *An' ye harm none, do what ye will.*

What ye send forth comes back to thee,
so ever mind the law of three,
Follow this with mind and heart,
Merry ye meet, and merry ye part.

This point is worth emphasizing: when it comes to ethics, do what you are comfortable with. This is your life, your power, your responsibility, and therefore your decision.

ENERGY WORK

Before learning how to work spells, create charms, or even send blessings, most witches are first taught the three basic techniques of energy work: centering, grounding, and shielding. Hannah Johnston, author of, *Children of the Green: Raising Our Kids in Pagan Traditions* explains, "energy is will, and will makes magic."[27] Practicing how to center, ground, and shield teaches us how to intentionally raise, release, and direct our energy. These skills enable us to effectively apply our will toward making magic.

BRUSHING UP ON THE BASICS

Before getting into teaching our kids about energy work, here is a quick refresher on these foundational techniques.

Grounding is when you allow excess energy to leave your body, typically through the soles of the feet or palms of the hand. After a working or ritual, you might feel a bit jittery, your mouth dry as dust, or tremors creeping under your skin as if you are cold. That is because you are full of energy. If you do not release it, these symptoms will only get worse. To ground energy, you can imagine roots extending from your feet, pushing deep into the ground. When energy cycles to your feet, it will be pulled down the roots instead of going back up into your body. There have been times when I was feeling overwhelmed from pent-up energy, so in addition to pushing energy into the ground, I imagined valves in the palms of my hands opening up and energy

---

27   Johnston, *Children of the Green*, 83.

pouring out of them like water from a faucet.

Grounding is a useful technique in other situations as well. Maybe life has been crazy, and you feel disconnected, or maybe you are confused about something. Let those roots reach into the ground and connect with the earth. Be mindful during this time, observing any changes that have occurred since you made the connection, aware of any sensations you feel or thoughts that float through your mind. Grounding allows you to be present, calms your body and mind, and is instrumental in meditation.

Young children are inherently connected to the world, so having them sit on the ground, playing with dirt, or gently combing the grass with their fingers will help them connect their energy to the earth with minimal effort. This will help to release some of their built-up energy that turns them into little whirlwinds wreaking havoc on the household.

Centering is fundamental to magic, so it is an important technique to master before attempting any blessings, spells, charms, etc. Without centering, you do not have anything to send out to manifest your intention. Centering is when you mindfully activate your power core, willing the energy to expand and cycle through your astral body. Making energy balls with your hands is a common centering exercise. You bring your attention to your power center— that is where your magic comes from. This is often in the belly (solar plexus) or in the chest (heart). Visualize a ball of light spinning around in the center of your core. As it spins, it grows, flowing outward from your center into your limbs, hands, feet, and head. When the energy is circulating from head to toe, start rubbing your hands together. Soon they will feel warm—this is because friction is building and drawing out energy as it flows through your hands. In your mind's eye, see a little ball of light take shape. As your hands move back and forth, round and round, they gradually pull apart as the ball of light grows. When the sphere is about the size of a baseball, you can play with it a bit, noticing any physical sensations you experience as you toss the ball from hand to hand.

Centering for little witchlings does not look much different than grounding. After they have stood with their toes in the dirt for a few moments, tell them to imagine they have roots that grow out of their feet and into the ground. If they reach far enough into the ground, they will find water, which their roots will suck up like a straw. Now direct their attention to the sky, telling them to pretend they are a tree and their arms are the branches. Have them lift their arms up over their head, reaching for the sun, palms up. With their eyes closed, ask them to imagine the sun's rays reaching down, down, down, until it touches their branches. Their hands are leaves, which soak up the light of the sun that nourishes their branches. Ask them if they feel the cool water climbing up their body and the warm light rolling down. Encourage them to use feeling words: "I feel tingly," or "I feel cool."

Shielding is a technique through which you expand and "harden" your aura, creating an energetic barrier around your body, protecting it from negative energies. Some traditions view "negative" energies as malicious and intent on harming. Personally, I take the alternative position, in that negative energies distract from the situation at hand. Say you are meditating on an intention—money, success, wealth, anything. Your family, however, is waiting for you to finish so you can all sit down to eat supper. As their hunger grows, their thoughts turn to you. The energy of their annoyance, their hunger, and their wish for you to stop meditating, finds its way to you. If you have your shield in place, you will not be affected. The shield is preventing these negative, or distracting, energies from interfering with your work.

To make the shield they have to push the light and water up their arms and have it jump from their palms like a fountain. It will stick to their aura, making it grow until it surrounds them like an egg that fits around them just enough so they can spin around with outstretched arms. Tell them to lower their arms, bringing them down in a big arc, and ask if they can feel their shield with their fingertips. If they have a hard time imagining this, it might help to gradually introduce them to the concept of the aura. Pull them into your lap and create your own shield, then direct their hand to the shield's edge. They should be able to feel a subtle difference between the air inside the shield, the shield itself, and outside the shield. I have done this work with my son. While he got the hang of grounding and centering, the aura and shield were tricky for him. To help him, I often had him sit in my lap and feel my aura, my shield, and reach out beyond the shield to see how the air felt different.

One of the most beneficial skills kids can learn in basic energy work is that of mindfulness. Mindfulness itself is a grounding technique, but not in the sense of connecting to the earth. Rather, one connects with the present moment. Mindfulness can be taught before, after, or in conjunction with basic energy techniques, as no one is too young to learn how to be present.

My son has hyperactive ADHD, so I often employ mindfulness techniques when we are taking a long car ride. He gets antsy, so I will simply cue him with questions until he is calm and present. I will ask him what he notices with each of the physical senses (*What do you hear? See? Taste? Feel?*). If that does not calm him, I will ask him how each sensation makes his heart feel, cuing him to be mindful of his emotions. The answers he will give are sometimes hilarious. For instance, he has told me that tasting the peanut butter that was on his sandwich at lunchtime makes him feel sad because he forgot to brush his teeth, or hearing the music playing in the car next to us makes him mad because, "they don't need to listen to music that loud."

Through energy work and mindfulness techniques, we encourage our kids to connect with their physical, emotional, and psychic senses, fostering an awareness of their place in the world. In their understanding of this web, they will come to see how their will, intention, thought, and action can make change—and can make magic.

TOOLS TO DIRECT ENERGY

There are several traditional magical tools that can direct energy, including wands, athames, swords, spears, or even an ordinary kitchen knife, if you are in a bind.

But the first tool we will talk about is really the only tool a witch may need: their finger. It is important to teach our kids that their body and mind are all they need for magic, as this is an empowering concept. It alleviates any feeling of panic for not having the 'right' tools. In fact, the best tools are those they are born with. Here are some fun exercises for your kids to learn how to direct energy with their fingers.

Keep in mind that energy work is draining. It can literally dehydrate you, so make sure you have water and maybe a snack on hand so they can eat and drink after the exercise.

Coloring the Wall

We are going to encourage coloring on the wall! With energy, that is. Stand before a wall with your child and center your energy. Feel it coursing through your body. Close your eyes and will the energy up your chest, through your shoulder and down your arm. When it reaches your hand, you may feel warmth or tingling. This is normal. Now raise your power hand (typically the hand you write with, or the hand you use to release energy), and extend your pointer finger.

With your minds eye, see the energy shoot out of your finger and toward the wall, as though you are using a laser pointer. What color is it? Try drawing a line, or making a scribble. Fun, isn't it? Try writing your name with energy on the wall. Change the color. Just see it gradually shift, starting from the point of your finger. The line of energy might change color like a mood ring. Go through various colors – red, orange, yellow, green, blue, purple, white. Write your name or draw some scribbles in each color, then pull the line back and ground the energy. You may have done this exercise when you were a newbie witch, but it is good to practice and familiarize yourself with it before teaching your kids.

Juggling

Creating balls of energy and tossing them from hand to hand is a great way to master directing energy. Juggling balls of energy is much easier than juggling real balls. Trust me, I have tried.

When you first start this exercise, start with warm-colored balls of light, such as red, orange, or yellow. The reason for this is because cool colors possess a higher amount of energy than warm colors. You will give yourself a nasty headache if you spend twenty minutes juggling white balls the first time around.

To create a ball, center your energy and direct it to your arms. Rub your hands together, slowly, in a circular motion. As you begin to feel tingling and warmth, your hands will start to separate. As they separate, see a small red ball in the center. It will become larger and brighter as you continue moving your hands in the circular motion. Keep doing this until the ball is about the size of a tennis ball. Then take the ball in one hand and set it down. See the ball in your mind's eye as you place it on your lap or the on table next to you. Now, make a second ball.

When that is done, take one ball in each hand and try juggling them. Stand up, feet hip width apart. Arms to your side, bent at the elbow with your palms up. Toss one ball up, tilting your hand as you flick your wrist so the ball will fly in an arc towards the opposite hand. After you release the first ball, toss the second. It may take a few tries to figure out timing. Gradually increase speed, tossing the balls a little higher, moving your arm at the elbow for the toss now rather than flicking your wrist.

When it is time to stop, take a ball in each hand and push them together, making one big ball. Hold the ball between your hands at chest level. Start grounding energy, seeing in your mind's eye the energy sliding down your body and into the ground. As the energy drains, it will move up your arms, through your shoulders, down the middle of your chest, and through the rest of your body. As the energy crawls your arms it will create a vacuum effect, pulling energy out of the ball through your palms. The ball will get smaller and dimmer, your hands coming together as this happens. Finally, the ball will disappear, and your palms will be resting against one another.

Once your child has established confidence in their energy exercises, you can begin incorporating tools into their routine. Discuss options with your little witch. What kind of tool do they want to use to direct energy? What should it be made of? Should you buy it, make it, or give them one of yours? Here are some tools to go over with them:

- **Wands**…A tool used to direct energy, often for the purpose of charging an object, or invoking a Higher Power. Wands are typically made of wood, crystal, clay, or plastic, with tips of crystal. Traditionally, the wand should be as long as the intended users' forearm.

- **Athame**… A dagger that is reserved for energy work. Wiccans traditionally use a double-edged blade with a black handle. Alternative options are a letter opener decorated like a dagger, an embellished butter knife, or a clay dagger with wire wrapped around the blade to aid with energy conduction.

- **Sword**…For kids, make one out of wood, paper mâché, or paper crafts.

Take into consideration your child's age, maturity, and personality when exploring the right tool for them. If they are not sure which tool they are drawn to, go to a dollar store and get them a plastic or foam sword or dagger. Or you can use items you find around the house to make a representation of each tool. The representations will not be very effective magical tools if they are not made of material that acts as an energy conductor, and that is okay – the point of getting a non-organic representation is to help them determine which tool is for them without spending a lot of money or time making the tool from natural material.

Representations

Should your child be partial to a tool made of non-organic material, then you may wish to repurpose items found around the house. Use creativity and artistic talent to transform the item into a magical tool. The time and energy spent turning an ordinary butter knife into a magical athame infuses the tool with your personal power. By the time you are done making it unique, you will not even have to enchant the object. You may want to create a ritual for your child in which they charge or bless the tool. It is important that you let your child take the lead when it comes to personalizing tools, as they will be the one using it. So I am not providing specific ideas for personalization.

When our little witchlings are ready for tools, it is a natural response to run to your magical tool chest to find tools to hand down to them. We must resist doing this, however. We must keep in mind that their practice is their own, so until they tell us what they need, we cannot assume we know.

INTRODUCING THE
MAGIC OF THE ELEMENTS

The magic elements- Earth, Air, Fire, Water, and Spirit - are a part of every aspect of life. So it is no wonder they play a crucial role in so many spiritual practices around the world, especially witchcraft. They are not only part of magic, though. As Monica Crosson says in, *The Magickal Family*, the elements are woven into all the realms and all life.

Many traditions of witchcraft use sacred tools to represent the four elements, and so the tools bring their power into our rituals and workings. They are such an inextricable part of witchcraft and Paganism, I recommend introducing your little witchlings to the elements as early as possible. Children as young as two years old can feel the stability of earth, the inspiration of air, the cleansing properties of water, and the invigorating warmth of fire. It does not matter if they do not fully understand how the powers can be utilized, or what the powers influence. That will come in time.

What is important is that they gain experience in connecting with these powers and move toward establishing a balanced relationship with the elements. Harmony with the elements creates harmony in life.

How you incorporate the elements into your child's practice should be based on your children. Each child is unique, so techniques that work for one child may not work for another. Introduce the elements in the time and manner that feels right for your family. To get you started, I have listed some activities that can help connect your child to each element. Feel free to try them as listed or modify them to better suit your kid's needs. I suggest practicing the technique yourself first and introducing it to your child once you are comfortable with it.

We will explore each of the elements - Earth, Air, Fire, and Water - including their qualities and associations. I will then offer suggestions for your kids to connect with each element, as well as provide a how-to for equipping your child with age-appropriate tools to wield the power of the elements.

But first, we will discuss the concept of predominant elements, which often correlate with a person's astrological sign. Knowing this will help you understand your children's behaviors and personalities, and will provide insight into ways to best introduce the elements. The predominant element affects a person's interests, preferred activities, and how they understand the world around them.[28] I will include the signs associated with each element, as well as their related personal characteristics.

Astrology and Predominant Elements

The earliest connection and communication we have with our children is physical. Dr. Hannah E. Johnston, in *Children of the Green: Raising our Kids in Pagan Traditions,* explains, "We show them our feelings, our hopes and expressions through our physical relationship with them"[29]. This is a stage that is body-centered, focusing on eating, sleeping, comfort, and family. Habits and routine are the foundation of their stability, safety, and well-being. As such, children are typically Earth-focused for their first five years of life.

The predominate element associated with each individual becomes apparent as the child grows beyond this phase. Some remain Earth-centered, while others shift to Air, Water, or Fire. A child's predominate element often correlates with their astrological sun sign. The sun signs that are associated with each element are as follows:

EARTH
•Taurus, Virgo, Capricorn•

Earth kids are loyal, dedicated, patient, and practical, driven by their goals and aspirations, with a predisposition for being stubborn, narrow-minded, and unimaginative.

Ways to Connect
With the Element of Earth

- Hug a tree. Focus on touch sensations, such as how the bark and leaves feel, or the roots, should there be any poking up through the ground. Have them look up into the branches to look for animals who live may there.

- Clay play. Using clay, play-doh, or even wet sand, let them play and encourage them to make things associated with Earth – land animals, plants, even rocks.

28   Monica Crosson, *The Magickal Family,*
29   Johnston, *Children of the Green,* 15

- Go on a nature walk.

- Play in a sandbox.

- Visit a petting farm.

AIR
•Gemini, Libra, Aquarius•

Air kids have a calm demeanor, innovative and intelligent minds, and are passionate about justice. Air kids have the tendency for unrealistic expectations and lofty aspirations, and can become impractical, cold, and flighty.

Ways to Connect
With the Element of Air

- Wishes on the wind. This is a versatile activity that can be done with balloons, bubbles, or dandelions with their fluffy seeds covering their heads. Instruct your child to close their eyes and whisper their wish into the object. When they are ready, blow or let it go. Tell them to watch their wish float away with the bubbles, balloon, or seeds.

- Writing and singing songs. My son loves singing songs. We sing about the day of the week, the things we see, and make up songs to describe the activity we are doing.

- Write or tell a story.

- Learn something new, such as the kinds of birds in the back yard, or the different kinds of clouds in the sky.

- Make wind chimes or a windsock. My son and I collect twigs, shells, even small gems to make wind chimes.

FIRE
•Leo, Aries, Sagittarius•

Fire kids are happy-go-lucky, honest, and are not afraid of anything. They are natural-born leaders, inspiring everyone around them. While it is great that Fire kids are self-confident and driven by their passions, this Fire, left untended, can make them domineering, self-centered, and reckless.

Ways to Connect
With the Element of Fire

- Watch a candle flame. Try to make it dance with a gentle breath or by waving of your hand (a safe distance from the flame), or just blow it out.

- Cooking fun. Have your child pay attention to how the pasta changes in the hot water, how the vegetables respond to the heated pan, or how the cookies change from the heat in the oven.

- Learn about animals that come in spring and summer and go away in the fall and winter. Find out why, where they go, and what they do during each season.

- Make a suncatcher.

WATER
•Cancer, Scorpio, Pisces•

Water kids are the artists, with creative minds inspired by their intuition. Water kids are naturally empathetic, so they are considerate and kind, but they do have the tendency to be compulsive, irrational, and oversensitive.

Ways to Connect
With the Element of Water

- Go swimming together.

- Give a bath, encouraging them to pay attention to how their bodies are cleaned. Tell them to think about things that worry them, scare them, or bother them in some way, and then imagine those worries being washed away with the dirt and grime.

- Adopt a pet fish, sea monkey, or hermit crab with your child.

- Create a feelings jar with them. Write out feelings on a piece of paper and collect them in a jar. At the end of each month, review and address the feelings. Keep the entries anonymous, so the whole family can enhance their empathy, imagining that they were the one with the feelings. Then work together to discuss the feelings. How can we make ourselves feel happy feelings more often, and what can we do to address not-so-happy feelings?

- Introduce divination. Start with oracle or Tarot cards. You can create a deck or find a family-friendly deck online to learn with your kids.

When little witchlings connect with and comprehend the four elements, the element of Spirit will be a natural next step. Their subconscious is already attuned to Spirit, so this element will feel familiar and natural to them. This is the key element to connect with and understand in witchcraft, so we want our kids not only to comprehend, but be comfortable connecting with, Spirit. Working the elements helps our children to understand that they are not *in* the world, they are *a part of it*. We want to teach them that they are as sacred as the sky above, the soil below, and all things in between.

WORKING
SPELLS

Working spells with your children can be as natural as magic. My son cannot comprehend laws of magic. He does not understand how to draw power, and he is not sure what "will" means, but he knows what it means to picture something in his head, and he knows he has power. That is enough.

With practice, encouragement, and openness, your kids can become deft at casting spells before they can even spell words. As they grow, you can gradually introduce them to complex laws and intricate correspondences. It is not something that can be rushed. This work should be enjoyed and used for practical reasons, like helping wildflowers grow in the same bed as rose bushes (as my son's wildflowers are). For those of you who do not have a green thumb, roses are selfish little plants that do not like to share their space. They will spread and choke out anything nearby. With magic, however, you can encourage your flowers to play nicely, as my son and I have.

Rather than discouraging them from believing in what they see or hear, or dismissing an active imagination, we should support their sensitive minds. Ask them to tell you about the little person in the tree or the funny creature near the bush. As with any stranger, advise your child to be cautious and respectful, and tell them to never go with any of these beings that you may not be able to see.

The best way to introduce magic is to get on your kids' level. Explain things in a way they can understand. My son sees the gods as superheroes like Thor and Iron Man. And I tell him he is exactly right. He knows that his power comes not from the gods, nor from the earth, but from within him. I tell him that he has power, just like the witch on Mickey Mouse, except witches are just like everyone else—and cannot, in fact, fly. I tell him that we do not use our power to scare people, like the witch scared Donald Duck in Mickey's House of Villains. We use it to help people, like how Mickey helps his friends. These are things he understands. Using examples from your children's favorite stories or movies will help them to firmly comprehend what they are doing with you and will, hopefully, teach them to be responsible with it.

Working spells with your kids can be incredibly rewarding. It brings you closer to your child and gives them a sense of confidence they will never find in school. They learn from a young age that they have the ability to make things happen, a magic they thought only possible in stories and movies. They learn to really pay attention to the world and to connect to the land and the elements. They will grow up knowing magic like they know how to read—it will come naturally and fluently. Your kids will be confident and self-sufficient but, at the same time, they will know their limits and when to ask for help. That is what we want for our kids anyway, magical or mundane, right?

ALL ABOUT AFFIRMATIONS

Affirmations are an excellent practice for kids, as they teach them the power of will, words, and visualization. Perhaps they are playing a new sport, or are learning an instrument. If they start each day by reminding themselves that they can do anything, they will quickly find that they learn new skills much easier, as they are training their mind to believe that they can.

Vision boards are excellent magical tools. Even non-magical people use them! They help you get clear on what you want and manifest your desire by displaying your goals in one aesthetically pleasing poster. While I say poster, you can use anything to make a vision board: poster board, a shoebox lid, a plank of wood, a broken-down cereal box. You can even make a digital vision board using social media, like Pinterest or a graphic design app, like Canva. As long as it helps you visualize your goals, you cannot go wrong.

When you use a vision board, a pathway is formed by crystallizing your goals and dreams. Making a vision board is quite simple and offers a teaching opportunity for your little witchlings.

Sit down with a pen and paper and make a list of goals you want to accomplish over the next year (or your preferred timeline). Then gather your supplies. Look up quotes, print pictures from the Internet, gather old magazines and cutout clips that inspire you and speak to your desires. Get markers, crayons, glitter, construction paper—whatever you and your kids feel compelled to use.

Once you have everything you need, look over your list and decide how you want to organize your board. I prefer to make mine chronologically. The things I want first go on top, and so on, down to the bottom of the board. Another way to do it is to divide your board into four sections, aligning to the cardinal directions. Draw a line diagonally from corner to corner, so the top aligns with the north, right with east, bottom with south, and left with west. This is a great way to help your kids become familiar with the cardinal directions and the elements.

Another aspect to keep in mind is color correspondences. You can write out or find a color chart from the Internet so your kids can refer to it, as needed. Color correspondences are useful for crafting any spell or ritual, so I encourage you to include them in the family vision board activity.

It helps to lay everything out before attaching items to the board to ensure they will all fit in a way that you like. That is the most important thing: it must be appealing for you. It does not matter if you look at your kid's board and cannot make heads or tails of it, as long as they know what it is about.

You can use an assortment of adhesives to stick the cutouts and such to the board, e.g., tape, glue, staples. Personally, I love using Mod Podge because it dries quickly, and you can swipe a thin coat over the top to give your board a nice shiny coat.

When the board is done, hang it somewhere you will see it regularly. Take a couple of minutes each day to just look at the board and envision reaching your goals, then go about your routine.

BACK-TO-SCHOOL
CHARMS AND SPELLS

Here some spells for you to teach your kids that will help them have a successful school year. These spells will, of course, require that they do the homework. They are not "easy A" spells. One spell will help your student pass a test, but only if they study. The second spell helps instill courage, whether it is needed for social or academic reasons. The third and final spell is for protection. It encompasses health and well-being, reducing risk of harm or illness.

Test Success Spell

Timing: Begin seven days before a test.

Ingredients:

- Cloth bag.

- Cinnamon (ground or stick)- for protection, success, and to repel negativity.

- Rosemary (dried) – for mental power and clarity.

- Sage (alternatives: almond or sunflower) – for wisdom.

- Bay laurel – for clarity.

- Crystals - for balance, calm, and clarity. Choose one or more of the following. Let your intuition guide you:

    ◊ *Amethyst*

    ◊ *Azurite*

    ◊ *Calcite*

    ◊ *Carnelian. (Recommended, because of the color and it aids in concentration, confidence, focus, motivation and decision making.)*

Seven days before the test: gather all the ingredients and lay them out on the altar or workspace. Take each item in turn. Hold it in your power hand and state what it is for (i.e., "This cinnamon helps me succeed, this carnelian stone aids with concentration, confidence, etc."). Then fill the bag with your objects, close it, and hold it in your hand. Imagine taking the test. Then picture getting it back with a good grade.

When you have a clear picture of passing the test, say or chant the following incantation over the bag:

> *Material studied is knowledge learned,*
> *A passing grade is what I've earned.*
> *When I take the test the right answer will come right to me,*
> *As I will, so mote it be.*

Study the material every night for the next five nights. Keep the pouch with you as you study, so it becomes imbued with the energy created from you studying. The night before the test you will not study because... But just before going to bed, review the material and repeat the incantation over the pouch. Keep it with you when you take the test – in your pocket, stuffed in your bra, in your shoe- whatever works. Be confident that you will pass. You have put in the magic and the work, so you will succeed.

Remind your child that they will have to study, but this pouch will help them retain the material and retrieve the right answers. They should understand that if they do not study, they will not pass. Magic only works if they do their part.

Courage Charm

Timing: Anytime.

Ingredients:

- Two lengths of ribbon in red and your favorite color. The length should be three times the circumference of your wrist or ankle, wherever you prefer to wear it.

Knot the ribbons together at the top, then wrap them around each other as you repeat the following chant:

> *Courage is what I need,*
> *to successfully accomplish the upcoming deed.*
> *I have all the tools, I have all the wits,*
> *and with my magic I guarantee success.*
> *One by one, two by two,*
> *I draw in courage to do what I must do.*
> *I draw the courage into me.*
> *As I will, so mote it be.*

Protection Charm

Timing: Any day, at noon.

Ingredients:

- Small box or pouch that can be kept in your backpack.

- Rosemary, for its protective and cleansing properties.

- Rose stem with thorns to repel harm.

- Dragons' blood resin to repel negativity and enhance spell work.

- Amethyst to enhance intuition and for protection.

- Crystal quartz to magnify spell work.

Put the ingredients in the pouch or box, focusing on the protective properties of each item. Hold them in your power hand. Envision a bubble of protection coming from the pouch, like a shield. Take the charm outside at noon and hold it in the sun. Let the light merge with the ingredients one at a time, until the whole charm is vibrating with the sun's warm, nurturing rays. Feel the light bind to the protective energy of the charm, and will the energy into the shape of a sphere. See the sphere, shining and protective, deflecting anything that means harm, and envision it growing until it is big enough to encompass your whole body. You may say a charm or chant, or just know that your container will hold this power until you remove the items. Wrapping a copper wire around the outside, making a closed circuit, will help contain the energies. They'll constantly cycle around and around, so it's unnecessary to recharge the charm. Without a closed circuit you should recharge it once a month.

FINAL THOUGHTS

It is called "working" magic because it takes *work*. It entails practice, dedication, and a lot of learning. Have patience and enthusiasm. It will go a long way in encouraging your kids to keep practicing, learning, and working at it. Let them know that you have to practice, too. Let them know that magic, like art, is not something that can be perfected. As sand in the sea, or the breeze through the air, it can grow, and it can strengthen. It is never lost, but it can weaken if there is nothing encouraging its growth. It is always a work-in-progress that will help your child grow and learn and have wonderful experiences in life.

Chapter 5

PRACTICES & TECHNIQUES: PSYCHISM & DIVINATION

"There is power in the act of seeking knowledge..."
-JASON OLSHAWSKY

MAGIC AND DIVINATION ARE THE ULTIMATE best friends – they are always together. It's advised to perform divination before working magic to ensure that you have not overlooked any unintended consequences of your actions. This applies to anyone who does magic, including children. This is why divination should be included in the curriculum for your child's magical education. Not only will this help them prepare for spell work, but it teaches your witchling to be aware of the world around them. They learn that their choices affect not only themselves, but other people too.

We will first explore what divination is. Then we will address psychic perception, how to help your child strengthen their psychic abilities, and methods of psychic protection. We will conclude with divination techniques that are appropriate for kids of all ages.

DEFINING DIVINATION

According to Silver Ravenwolf's *To Ride a Silver Broomstick*, divination is, "The art of using magickal [*sic*] tools and symbols to gather information from the collective unconscious on the nature of people, places, things, and events in the past, present, and future"[30] Per Raymond Buckland, divination is, "being aware of the forces at work that will bring about a probable result in the future."[31] Divination is a practice that allows you to obtain information that cannot be acquired by mundane means. In addition to being a practice, divination is an art, which means that it is something that can always be improved upon. The longer one practices divination, the more refined one becomes in reading. My son is four, so by the time he is old enough to truly work spells, he will be fluent with divination and able to cast wisely.

THE CLAIRS:
STRENGTHENING PSYCHIC ABILITIES

Psychic ability is the "processing of extrasensory perception that doesn't rely on primary sensory information about one's environment."[32] We perceive this information through our psychic senses- using our 'clairs'. Clair, French for clear, is the prefix of each name of the psychic senses. They are:

- **Clairvoyance**, "clear seeing", perceived as pictures or sequences of events that you see in your mind's eye.

- **Clairaudience**, "clear hearing", perceive information in the form of sound – speech, music, etc., - hearing them in your mind.

- **Claircognizance**, "clear knowing", often referred to as intuition, is when you "just know" something – you didn't see it, read it, hear it, or otherwise, but you know it nonetheless. This is one of my dominant clairs…it used to get me into trouble when I was a child. My parents would discipline me for eavesdropping, as that was the only way they could logically explain how I knew about things I shouldn't have known.

- **Clairtangency**, "clear touch", a somewhat complex psychic sense and often confused with clairsentience. It is a psychic perception that involves touching a person or object with your hands. It may present as

---

30   Silver Ravenwolf, *To Ride a Silver Broomstick* (Woodbury: Llewellyn Publications, 2017), 25.
31   Raymond Buckland, *Buckland's Complete Book of Witchcraft* (Woodbury: Llewellyn Publications, 2017), 157.
32   Mat Auryn, *Psychic Witch*, (Woodbury: Llewellyn Publications, 2020), 11, Kindle.

palpable psychic sensations on or within the body, (i.e., you learn that your child has an earache by touching their head and feeling a sudden pain or pressure in your ear). Gaining knowledge by physically touching something is a practice referred to as psychometry, (i.e., holding a necklace to gain information about the person who owns it, touching an artifact you unearthed by happenstance, to learn more about the object, the land, and/or the people who have dwelt).[33]

- **Clairsentience**, "clear feeling", is the psychic perception of physical sensations within the body.[34] If you are performing a mediumship reading, for example, you may learn how the spirit died by feeling pain or pressure in a part of your body that corresponds with their cause of death – i.e. tightness in your chest that tells you they died from a heart attack.

In addition to these 'primary' clairs, there is clairalience (smell), clairgustance (taste), and clairempathy (emotion).[35] These minor clairs are no less important, of course, but provide a rather limited amount of information, as opposed to one of the clairs from the list above. People typically have one psychic ability, or *clair*, that is naturally stronger than the others. You could take the time to work with your child on identifying their strongest clair, but I suggest working on all of them. If your eyesight is much stronger than your hearing, would you want to work on strengthening only your eyes? No, you would want to keep your eyesight strong and improve your hearing as well. It is the same with psychic abilities.

One does not necessarily need to have strong psychic abilities to perform divination efficiently. However, psychic abilities provide more information about that which is learned from a divination reading, giving the witch insight that would not have been obtained were the witch to have relied on the divination tool's generally accepted interpretations. For example, interpreting a Tarot reading based purely on the little booklet's definitions is not as effective as including our own psychic impressions along with years of study on the divination form. Tressabelle, of the Ozark

---

33   Mat Auryn, *Psychic Witch*, 62.
34   Mat Auryn, *Psychic Witch*, 10.
35   Mat Auryn, *Psychic Witch*, 10.

Pagan Mama blog, explains that, before starting divination lessons, you can start to strengthen their psychic abilities simply "by paying heed to their "hunches" or "gut feelings" when they arise, and creating a safe environment for your child to express such feelings of knowing... a greater importance for honing a child's intuition than just for learning divination- a child who trusts her/his own thoughts and feelings have a greater sense of self worth, self love, and connectedness."[36]

Here are a few ways to help your child strengthen build their psychic abilities. I recommend obtaining a special notebook or journal, so you or your child can keep track of the exercises and their results, enabling you to track their progress, determining which areas they excel at and what they need extra help with.

Find the Ace

Ellen Dugan recommends this in her book, *The Natural Psychic*, sharing how she did it with her own children. All you need is a deck of playing cards. Pull the Ace of Spades, the Ace of Hearts, and the Ace of Diamonds from the deck and set aside the rest of the cards. The Ace of Spades is bold, usually depicted with a large spade on the card. This is the card you want to find, so study it carefully, crafting it in your mind. The other two aces are red, so the Ace of Spades stands out against them. Lay the cards out on a flat, sturdy surface, face down. Mix them up so you do not know which card is where, then arrange them in a line. Hold your hands out and slowly move them over the cards. When you feel that you have found the Ace of Spades, flip it over. What is great about this exercise is you can utilize essentially any psychic ability. You can make it challenging, declaring that the player may only rely on clairvoyance, or clairaudience, or clairtangency to find the Ace.

---

36   Tressabelle, "Divination for Kids," Ozark Pagan Mama Blog, October 6, 2013, https://tressabelle.wordpress.com/2013/10/06/divination-for-kids/

> ## *Dream Journal*
>
> Part of psychic training entails learning and deciphering the symbols your subconscious uses to communicate messages. A dream journal is an excellent way to learn and record these symbols. I use a three-ring binder as a dictionary of my dream symbols. This will help your child develop a deeper understanding of him or herself, which empowers them to make wiser choices regarding what is best for them and the path they want to take as they grow into adulthood.

PSYCHIC PROTECTION

Before diving into divination, I recommend you first teach your little witchling how to protect themselves, and then work with them on developing their psychic skills. Every person is psychic, but people typically have one ability that is stronger than others. Because psychic protection entails visualization and projection, I suggest that you begin with those skills. The stronger their psychic abilities get, the more they will need the protection. The protection will be stronger if their psychic abilities are stronger. It is all related.

The way you approach psychic protection depends largely upon your child. My son has a creative and vivid imagination, so I started by supporting him in his belief in his imaginary friend— a dragon the size of my car. From the moment he "introduced" me to his fiery friend, I encouraged him to see his pal as his protector, as well as playmate. It was not long after that I taught my son how to create a shield.

He knows he has power, so it was almost effortless to convince my son that he can create an invisible bubble around his body to protect himself. I told him that sometimes, people will be jealous of his "thinking power," and they will try to make him think badly about himself to take away his power. I felt that this was the best way to describe it in terms he can understand. I did not want to scare him by telling him about energetic vampires and other unseemly entities. I also do not want him to think that everything and everyone is friendly. It is just not safe. I told him that if he gets strange or scary thoughts, he can put up his bubble and the bad thoughts will stop. We practice our bubbles every day. I definitely recommend teaching your child how to shield, (and it would not hurt if they had an imaginary protector either). But trust your instincts and approach the subject in a way that is most suitable for your child.

DIVINATION METHODS

While any method of divination could be taught to children, there are certain methods that are easier for kids of all ages. I want to reiterate the advice I offered in Chapter 3, which is that introducing children any aspect of witchcraft, be it magic or divination, should be creative, fun, and interesting. We want our children to know that they are not obligated to learn divination, that you will not be disappointed if they do not want to try it, or if they want to stop because they are uncomfortable.

Scrying

Scrying is the traditional art of gazing into a reflective surface, such as a crystal ball or a bowl of water, to obtain psychic messages. This technique is not limited to reflective surfaces, however. One way to scry is by gazing at the clouds. The diviner deciphers the answer to a question by interpreting the shapes of the clouds. The unconscious attributes meaning to the shapes and sends the message to your conscious. This method is a great starter for kids because it gets them outside and connecting with nature, they develop their symbol dictionary, and gain confidence in their intuition. There is never a wrong answer with scrying, which really boosts kids' confidence. My son loves cloud gazing. By laying in our backyard, pointing to clouds and talking about what they look like and how they make us feel, he is subconsciously developing a set of associations to various symbols. When he gets older, these associations will return to him, so scrying will come naturally to him.

Dowsing

Dowsing is a technique wherein the direction of a pointer is interpreted in response to a question. A common form of dowsing is the use of a pendulum, which is typically used to answer yes-or-no questions. What is great about this technique is that your child can create the pendulum by attaching a stone, crystal, ring, or anything with a little weight to it to a string or chain. Once the pendulum is made, it must be calibrated. Hold it out in front of you so the pointer is hanging straight down. First, instruct the pendulum to show you "yes," with a particular movement. Wait for it to stop and then instruct it to show you "no." Pendulums can also be used to help locate items by swinging in the direction of the lost object.

Runes, Ogham, &
Magical Alphabet Stones

This method entails the use of a set of stones, chips, or staves that are inscribed with symbols. Each symbol has a specific meaning, and they are read either by drawing them from a pouch or by tossing them on the floor or a padded surface. The stones that land closest to you, or furthest away from the rest of the pile, are chosen to be interpreted. Younger kids will need help with this at first, especially when it comes to learning what each symbol means. You could use Runes, Ogham, or you can come up with a completely new magical alphabet. Creating these stones is a large part of the fun. With clay and inscribing tools, or stones and paint or permanent markers, you can make your own set. The process of creating and inscribing the stones is a great way for the child to familiarize him-or-herself with the various symbols.

Serpent Stones

Serpent stones are a set of three stones, one saying, "yes," another saying, "no," and a stone that usually says, "maybe." In my opinion, this is a great way to start divination with younger children. Even if the child cannot read yet, they can learn the stones by their shape and color. They ask a question and then draw a stone for an answer. Simple, quick, and efficient.

Seasonal Wisdom:
DIY Oracle Cards

Your kids can make their own oracle deck, but this activity is also designed to help your child learn the land around your home, and particularly that of the plant life. The process involves getting to know native plants and then creating an oracle card for each one. Decide which areas you want to explore for plants, and how many cards you want to add each season. Allow the deck to grow at your child's pace. Start small, with 2-4 plants. The first couple of trips will be dedicated to finding the plants. The following weeks will for observing and forging a friendship with the plants. The cards will be made at the end of the season, when your kid has a strong connection to their plant pals.

Here is how you do it. For your first 'finding walk,' bring a notebook, something to write with, a camera, a local plant life guide (or your phone, which would provide access to both). Before you begin, go over the plan with your kids, (i.e., where you will go, how far, how long). Then set an intention for the walk: to find 'plant pals' who will be featured on the cards of your new oracle deck.

Be sure to keep your senses open and receptive, so you do not miss any psychic messages a plant may be sending you. Encourage your children to do the same. If your kiddo is really young, chances are they will run over to a plant or flower without even realizing why. That is a good indication that the spirit of that plant is calling out to them.

First, take a photo of the plant and jot down why you approached it. Have your child tell you qualities or characteristics they notice about it. Be supportive and enthusiastic. If they say that they chose that particular rose bush because a gnome lives amongst the roots, then write that down. If they said they chose that fruit tree because it reminded them of an elephant, then write that down. Give your child time to acquaint themselves with the plant and then continue on your route. If you only find one plant on the first walk, that is okay. You have an entire season, so do not rush it.

After you have found the plant pals for the season, change up the times and days you visit them. Make notes on how the plant changes based on the time of day, and how it changes over time. The more your kid gets to know the plants, the more the plants will reveal to them. You can encourage the conversations if you feel called, such as asking your child what magic powers the plant has, what the plant thinks the purpose of life is, or what it thinks about a particular situation or issue. Take notes on everything! You never know what will prove useful.

When the season is coming to a close and the plant starts to transition to a new phase of life, you can sit down with your kids to make the cards. Either print pictures to paste onto the front of the card, or have your kids draw pictures. I would recommend the latter. If you ask them to draw the flower and they draw a rainbow, by all means, keep the rainbow! Just ask them why they drew it and include their response in the meaning you attribute to the card in your guidebook.

When the cards are done, encourage your children to use them often. The littles may not want to do more than stick the card to the fridge or tape it to their wall. But as they get older, they will use the cards for guidance and advice. I strongly recommend laminating or putting a protective cover on the cards. Even covering it with clear scotch tape will suffice. You just want to prevent the card from getting damaged, because this deck will be one that your child will treasure and will likely use often as they get older. It may also become a treasured keepsake for you as the parent.

FINAL THOUGHTS

Choosing which method of divination to start with in your family can be intimidating. My advice is do not overthink it. What does your gut tell you? What does your child like to do for fun? If they are daydreamers who like to lay on the ground and watch the clouds or the stars, then scrying is likely the best choice. Do they like to draw? Is your child an earth sign, grounded and pensive? Then working with runes, Ogham, or creating a system of symbols and applying it to handmade cards or clay stones will be their preferred method. Is your child pragmatic and direct? If your kid likes direct yes-or-no answers, then dowsing or serpent stones will likely be their favorite.

Keep in mind, "Child rearing is ruled by parental instinct"[37]. While my advice is well-researched and personally tested, that does not necessarily mean it is what will be best for your children. I hope that what I have to offer is helpful, but always go with your instinct.

---

37 Emyme, "Magical Prep for the Nursery," In *Llewellyn's 2020 Witches' Companion*, (Woodbury: Llewellyn, 2019), 225, Kindle.

Chapter 6

PRACTICES & TECHNIQUES: EARTH-BASED SPIRITUALITY

"...Studying nature is learning divinity..."

-DIANE BAKER, *CIRCLE ROUND*

S PIRITUALITY REFERS TO SOMETHING "BEYOND THE self".[38] Belief can be in a deity, or many deities, or it could be in the power of the interconnectedness of the world. Psychologically speaking, to differentiate between spirituality and religiousness, spirituality has been defined as an "inner belief system that the universe and all people are connected in ways we can't see."[39] I have tried to keep this chapter as inclusive as possible, doing my best to keep from leaning towards one belief system over another.

---

38   Elizabeth Scott, "What is Spirituality?", Very Well Mind, November 27, 2020, https://www.verywellmind.com/how-spirituality-can-benefit-mental-and-physical-health-3144807
39   Teri Cettina, "Teaching Spirituality to Kids," Parenting, December 19, 2010, https://www.parenting.com/child/teach-spirituality-kids/

THE IMPORTANCE OF ATTENDING TO CHILDREN'S SPIRITUAL NEEDS

It is important to attend to children's spiritual needs, for many reasons. Significantly, a person's sense of identity is strongly tied to their spiritual beliefs. Researchers at the University of British Columbia found that spirituality gives children a sense of meaning and value, and helps them to develop, "deep, quality relationships." Studies show a strong correlation between these factors and happiness, indicating that kids are happier overall when they have a strong spiritual foundation[40]

According to Peggy Jenkins, Ph.D., of *Nurturing Spirituality in Children,* establishing a spiritual life for children helps them to understand that they live, " in a mental and spiritual world and that whatever is in their lives is the material expression of their beliefs."[41] In other words, children learn to see the world as an effect, rather than the cause, further solidifying witchcraft's emphasis on the importance of personal accountability, the power of the mind, and the magic that they inherently possess. Jenkins explains that every physical law is mirrored in the realms of mind and spirit (sounds familiar, right? *As above, so below, as within, so without...*).

EARTH-BASED SPIRITUALITY

Earth-based spirituality is based on the belief that the 'greater power' comes from the Earth, or from the spirit of the Earth. Animism, the belief that everything in nature has a soul or spirit, is a concept that we often find as an integral aspect of an earth-based spirituality. A reverence for nature and the belief in the power of the Earth is an ancient concept. It is the foundation of shamanism, which is believed to be the oldest form of religion on the planet. Earth-based spirituality may entail a belief in deities, Otherworldly beings, or personified forms of nature spirits. The source of power is something that I feel that we should allow our children to determine as they grow and get older.

---

40   Springer Science+Business Media, (2009, January 12). "Spirituality Is Key to Kids' Happiness, Study Suggests," *ScienceDaily*, Retrieved March 1, 2022, from www.sciencedaily. com/releases/2009/01/090108082904.htm
41   Peggy Jenkins, *Nurturing Spirituality in Children,* (New York: Atria Books, 2008), Section: Laying the Foundation, Kindle.

As parents, we establish the foundational beliefs of earth-based spirituality, in that we teach our children to revere the interconnectedness of people and nature, emphasizing the fact that we are just as much a part of nature as the trees, the flowers, the critters in the yard.

A foundation in earth-based spirituality will create a sense of belonging in our kids, not only amongst other people, but to the earth and all who dwell here. Encouraging our children to practice kindness to all - human, animal, and plant life alike - and doing work that helps people, animals, or the land, will lay the bricks of this foundation.

Kids-Only Altar

If you have an altar at home, you may have asked your children not to touch it. To validate their beliefs and to make them feel special enough to have a sacred space of their own, help them set up an altar just for them. You could make one for each child, or create one 'kids only' altar for all of them. Or consider a family altar in a communal room, and a small altar for each child in their bedroom(s).

To get them started you can make suggestions for things to put on it, such as representations of the elements, depictions of how higher-powers present themselves to the child, colors that correlate with the season, etc. Set an example of proper altar care by allowing them to watch you clean and update your altar, or establish a certain time of day as a 'spiritual time out,' providing you and your kids time to spend at the altar, or to meditate and connect with Spirit.

CONNECTING WITH THE EARTH: SEASONAL CELEBRATIONS

The Wheel of the Year is a cycle of festivals celebrated by modern-day Pagans comprised of four solar holidays (solstices and equinoxes), and four seasonal holidays (the start of each season). It is largely based on the Celtic calendar, with influences from other ancient calendars from surrounding pre-Christian cultures. It is often associated with Wicca, but I like the concept because it helps to ground me in the year. It is so easy to lose track of time, especially when you are a parent. How many times have you thought, "It's his birthday *already?!*" Or, "Oh man, winter holidays are right around the corner!"

Being mindful of the seasons helps to slow down time and enables you to be mindful and grateful for each day. Celebrating seasonal festivals helps our kids learn the land, forging a connection to the flora and fauna of the area, and provides them with a sense of stability. They know what to expect, and when to expect it.

Teaching your little witchlings about the Wheel of the Year enlightens them about so much more than the changing of the seasons, though. They learn that change is the only constant and can accept it with an open mind and heart. We are showing our kids how to use their psychic abilities, how to commune with spirits of nature, and, most importantly, how to pay attention.

Witches are wise because they listen, think things through, and they use all of their senses—both physical and nonphysical. When I feel the seasonal energies shift, the first thing I do is redecorate my home. My entire home is an altar honoring the season. By designing activities that encourage my son to connect with nature, I provide him with the tools he will need to honor the Wheel in his own unique way as he grows.

THE WHEEL OF THE YEAR

The festivals, or holidays, of the Wheel of the Year are as follows:

- December 21: Winter Solstice, or "Yule"

- February 1: First signs of Spring, or "Imbolc" (cross-quarter day)

- March 21: Spring Equinox, or "Ostara"

- May 1: May Day, or "Beltane" (cross-quarter day)

- June 21: Summer Solstice, or "Litha"

- August 1: First Harvest, or "Lughnasadh" (cross-quarter day)

- September 21: Autumn Equinox, or "Mabon"

- October 31-November 1: New Year, or "Samhain" (cross-quarter day)

I would like to note that the festivals may fall on or near the dates provided, depending on the year. For the exact date of the holiday, I suggest looking for an updated calendar of the Wheel of the Year.

December 21

The winter holidays - Yule, Christmas, and various others - are about family, gratitude, gift-giving, and finding the Light to guide you through the darkest night and celebrate the rebirth of the sun.

For my family, December 21, is reserved for gift giving. So I am going to share with you how I have incorporated Santa into my family's celebrations. Then I will share a fun, crafty activity you can do with your kids, as crafts are always a part of any holiday celebration in my home.

My son first heard about Santa on television. He has since come home with Santa stories from classmates. When he first asked about Santa my mind drew a blank, and then thoughts flooded in, all vying for my focus:

"Tell him it's a myth!"

"No, include Santa!"

"Tell him he's a spirit!"

"No, tell him he's dead!"

"Ignore the question! Tell him to look over there, and when he looks away, run!"

I took a deep breath, quieted my mind, and looked at my son, trying to determine what it was he wanted to hear. That may have been an invasion of my son's privacy, but honestly, I did not know what to do! Santa is a Christian thing, right? Is he a scare tactic - a method of parenting I actively avoid? But looking into my son's eyes, I could see that he really wanted Santa to be real.

I am not sure if parenting helps me as a writer, or if because I am a writer, I am a creative parent, but either way I was able to come up with a speech on the spot, telling him about Santa but fluffing up the tale with details that aligned with our beliefs. This is what I told him:

Santa Claus is a special spirit, a spirit of gifts! Every year, shortly after the winter solstice—remember that's when Father Sun comes back to Mother Earth—Santa climbs into a sleigh that is pulled by magic reindeer. These reindeer can fly! They fly all over the world and bring presents to all the little girls and boys that write Santa a letter. This is a special letter. It's your thank-you letter for the whole year! You write down things you are most thankful for, and because you appreciate so much, Santa will give you one more thing to say "thank you" for!

My son has heard this little story countless times by now, and still his eyes get wide, and he claps and jumps with excitement. I did not want to tell him Santa is just for "good" kids because *all* kids are good. Sure, some make poor choices, but everyone makes mistakes now and then. Instead, I thought it best to emphasize that he should be thankful. You are welcome to use this story and adjust it as needed to better fit your family's values.

My family starts the winter season, which is marked by the first real snowfall after Samhain, by cleaning the house. Well, I clean the house and my son spends the time in his room playing with toys he forgot he had because they were shoved under the bed, stuck in the couch cushions, or in a kitchen cabinet. After the house is clean and our autumn decorations are packed away, we bundle up in warm clothes, put our winter boots on, grab some baskets, and head outside to scavenge for fallen treasures. We collect pine cones, sticks, pine needles, and anything else that has fallen from trees or bushes. We go until our baskets are full—or until we are too cold to keep going—and then we bring back our treasures and put them on the art table. We pull out our craft supplies and decide what we are going to make to decorate the house for winter.

One of the reasons I love Yule is because it's such an energetically charged time of year, providing the opportunity to work towards a number of intentions:

- Honoring of and expression of gratitude for family, loved ones, hearth and home, life and career. Showing one another love and respect and expressing gratitude for life, love, happiness, etc. This is often carried out through gift-giving and performing charitable acts.

- The celebration and/or evaluation of personal achievements and growth, followed by acknowledgment and acceptance of one's abilities – their strengths and areas in need of improvement. Seeing and accepting yourself for who you truly are brings a deep sense of peace to the soul and paves the way for self-love.

- Introspection and reflection, determining what one wants or needs to determine realistic, attainable goals.

- Cleansing/banishment of energies and replacement or recharging of protections in and around the home, enhancing the feelings of calm and comfort to reduce the stress and chaos of the winter holidays.

DIY Yule décor can attract and enhance the energies your family wants to focus for the season. Some activities/décor are rather limited in the kinds of intentions they can help manifest, while others are extremely versatile, comprised of ingredients that correspond to any kind of intention, or they are customizable, their characteristics designed for a specific intention.

One such activity is salt dough ornaments. They work well with just about any magical intention and can be personalized in any number of ways. I like to design them around the magical properties of salt – cleansing, banishment, protection. They could work towards any intention, though, because they can be formed into any shape and decorated with any color, shape, or size, and then adorned with crystals and herbs.

Salt Dough Ornament Recipe

Below is a salt dough ornament recipe from *The Magickal Family*, by Monica Crosson[42].

- 1 c. Flour

- 1/2 c. Salt

- 1/2 c. Cinnamon

- 2/3 c. Water

- Wax paper

- Holiday cookie cutters

- Needle or nail (something to poke hole in ornaments to string them)

- Craft bells

- Hot glue gun

- Ribbon, string, heavy thread (something to hang the ornaments)

---

42   Monica Crosson, *The Magickal Family: Pagan Living in Harmony with Nature*, (Woodbury: Llewellyn Publications, 2017), Kindle.

Mix the flour, salt, cinnamon, and water together. Roll the dough about ½ inch thick between two sheets of wax paper. Using your cookie cutters, cut out your ornaments. Make a hole at the top to thread them onto ribbon later. Let them dry for 24 hours. This recipe makes about 12 ornaments, so if you want more, double the recipe, or halve it if you want less.

When your ornaments are hard, you can paint them if you wish or leave them as they are (usually a nice rustic color). If you wish to paint them, I would wait until *after* gluing the bells on, especially if you use acrylic paint. I once painted and then glued, and the bells fell off, leaving a spot where the paint tore away with the glue. Use your hot glue gun to attach the craft bells, then poke the thread, ribbon, or string through the hole and tie it off, so you can hang them on your Yule tree (or on a hook around the house).

February 1

Imbolc is a cross-quarter day, the midway point between winter solstice and spring. While it may not be visible yet, there is life starting to move under the snow and ice, deep beneath the land. The sun is starting to rise earlier and set later in the day. In *Llewellyn's 2020 Sabbats Almanac*, "The Old Ways: Predicting the Weather", article contributor Charlynn Walls explains that, "Imbolc is the first festival after the longest night of the year. The days are slowly getting longer and the impatient wait for spring is in full swing. Imbolc heralds the return of the sun, a time when the Goddess returns to speed the way for spring." [43]

Historically, Imbolc is an agrarian holiday. The translation of *Imbolg* (Irish word for Imbolc) means "in the belly," or "in the milk." *Oimelc*, another name for the day, translates to "ewe's milk." So, anyone who is not an animal husbandry enthusiast probably will not be thrilled to know that the sheep are lactating. As J.D. Hortwort puts it, "Try to explain the significance of that to someone not accustomed to the intricacies of animal husbandry . . . Fortunately, if Modern Pagans don't always grasp the idea of sheep coitus, they usually have a good understanding of the nature of seeds." [44]

---

43   Charlynn Walls, "The Old Ways: Predicting the Weather", in Llewellyn's 2020 Sabbat Almanac, ed. Annie Burdock (Woodbury: Llewellyn Publications, 2019), 97-101, Kindle.
44   J.D. Hortwort, "Imbolc," in *Llewellyn's 2019 Sabbats Almanac*, ed. Aaron Lawrence (Woodbury: Llewellyn Publications, 2018) Section 3, article 1, Kindle.

The nature of seeds is a good way to introduce Imbolc to your kids (unless you want to explain sheep coitus). My son helps me garden in the spring and summer, so he knows that once the seed is put into the soil and given water, sunlight, and lots of love, it will sprout and bring forth a flower or an herb for our kitchen. I tell him that magic happens under the soil, that it is a spark that starts life, and that this spark causes the seed to open and turn into roots. So, Imbolc is the time of year when that spark lights.

Speaking of light, the whole premise of Groundhog Day is that if the day is bright and clear, and Phil sees his shadow, then we have another six weeks of winter. If the day is gray and gloomy, however, there is no shadow to be seen. This means that winter is on its way out, and spring is right around the corner. The tradition dates back to an old English folk song:

> *If Candlemas be fair and bright,*
> *Come Winter, have another flight.*
> *If Candlemas brings cloud and rain,*
> *Go Winter and come not again.*

We celebrate Imbolc to remind ourselves that winter is coming to an end. It gives us a little boost to hold on until spring breaks free from the icy grips of winter. It allows us to forget about the difficult times by focusing on the good times to come. There are a number of ways to celebrate, and I will share with you a few that are family-oriented.

Making Your Own Basket

Homemade baskets can be used to hold offerings to Bridget, often associated with Imbolc, as decoration, or to fill with things that remind you of spring. It can be kept on a shelf in a prominent spot in your home. My son and I fill ours with seeds and other things that symbolize the season and we keep it on my altar.

What you will need:
- Bowl to use as a mold
- Plastic wrap
- Tacky glue
- Raffia

Cut strips of raffia and lay them out by size. Pour some glue into a dish so you can dunk the raffia into the glue. Wrap the bowl with plastic wrap, so every inch of the bowl is completely covered.

Cover the bottom of the bowl with raffia. Dunk the raffia strip in glue so it is completely saturated, then lay the pieces over the bottom, crisscrossing to keep the bottom sturdy. Do not worry about pieces that stick over the top, you can trim them later. When the bottom is covered, wrap pieces around the sides of the bowl. You may want to add another piece that goes from one side, under the bottom, and up the other side, in a cross shape, so the bowl remains sturdy and in shape. Put the bowl aside to dry and leave for 24 to 48 hours. When the bowl is completely dry, trim the top, and gently pull the basket away from the plastic wrap. Ta-da! You have a handmade basket! Possible offerings include crystals, seeds, and fresh plant clippings (just be sure to ask the plant permission first).

GroundHog Day Prediction Party

If you are in North America, you might look forward to Groundhog Day. You can spend Imbolc preparing for a Groundhog Day prediction party.

Have your kids draw or color groundhogs to hang up around the room. Then help them make a poster where everyone can mark their prediction. Make a dessert or something fun with your kid to serve as a prize for those who made the correct prediction. Then tune in to the Groundhog Day festival on February 2!

Protection Perfume

This is not a traditional Imbolc activity. I got this idea from Erin Rovin's book, *Little Laveau: Bayou Beware!* I love Erin Rovin's Little Laveau series, which are excellent for little witchlings and non-magical children alike. They are heart-warming, exciting, and inspiring stories, accompanied by delightful and detailed illustrations. In addition to magical themes woven throughout the stories, each installment of the Little Laveau series includes a set of easy-to-follow instructions on how to do one or more of the magical workings/spells included in the story.

In *Little Laveau: Bayou Beware*, Little Laveau learns about "Gram's Protection Perfume Recipe". Gram advises Little Laveau of the best route to take in the travels she would embark upon that evening, telling her that she should not take the shortcut through the "Dark Forest". The Dark Forest is spooky and disorienting, and, unless you knew the forest well, it would be easy to lose your way, especially after the sun sets. Gram informs Laveau that she knew this because, when she was about Laveaus' age, she got lost in the woods. When Little Laveau inquired as to how she found her way out of the woods, Gram replied, "[m]agic."

So, this got me thinking. She was stuck in the dark, as we are stuck in the dark of winter. This perfume was used to bring her into the Light, and it can help us find our way into the Light. We can use it to protect ourselves against illness, depression, restlessness, or anything that may come along with the barren winter months.

Per "Grams' Protection Perfume Recipe," you "[s]tart with rose petal oil for beauty…a drop of lavender oil for calming…a drop of basil oil for healing."[45] I would mix these into a base oil of almond or coconut and put it into a little spray bottle that you can keep handy. You can spritz it onto your child's backpack before they go to school, or spritz your car before you have to drive in less-than-ideal conditions.

Cardboard Candles

Since kids and fire are not a good combination, you can make candles with your kids out of toilet paper rolls and construction paper. You will need scissors, tape, and markers.

Start with construction paper—red, orange, and yellow—and cut out flame shapes. Next, take a new sheet of construction paper—any color you like—and wrap it around the toilet paper roll. Tape or glue the flames to the top, and voila! Kid-safe candles! You can help your kids write on the candles wishes or blessings they would like to receive from Bridget.

March 21

The Spring Equinox, or Ostara, is one of my favorite holidays to celebrate with my kids. I tell my son about the Spring Bunny and how the

---

45   Erin Rovin, *Little Laveau: Bayou Beware*, (New Orleans: First River Road Press, 2018), 35.

goddess sends the bunny out to breathe life into the land again. I explain that eggs represent the start to life, which is why we use them to both decorate our home and magically encourage spring to come. My parents are Greek Orthodox, and Easter is important to them. It has taken a few years, but they have finally got on board with me in calling the Easter Bunny the Spring Bunny. If they insist on leaving eggs filled with candy for my son, they have to at least call it the same thing I do, right?

The tale of Ostara is that a rabbit sought to win the favor of the Germanic spring goddess, Ostara, by decorating and presenting eggs. To this day, he still hides eggs about in her honor. But Ostara is more than family gatherings, sugary treats, or debating with your Greek stepmother whether the Easter Bunny should be called the Easter Bunny.

Ostara is the perfect season to start telling your children about how life begins because it is all around us. It is about life—new life—about awakening and warmth. It is an opportunity to tutor your children about love, the miracle of reproduction, and, of course, the chance to make magic. Bunnies, cats, chickens, sheep, animals small and large are reproducing, and this is why we honor that new life by decorating the house with eggs. The egg is the starting point; it represents the spark that ignites the fire that is life.

I use the opportunity of new life springing up around us to tell my son of how life is started. I say that humans are not much different than seeds in the garden. Some people have eggs inside them, and some people can put seeds in them. As of yet, he has not asked for more detail and I am fine with that. When he is older, I will tell him more.

Growing up, my parents treated sex as though it was shameful and secretive. I cannot blame them, it is how they were raised. I have a different approach, however. In my house, there are no cutesy names for genitals. I have a vagina, and my son has a penis and scrotum. It is what they are called. This is now the recommended approach, as it helps keep children safe when they are able to use words for their bodies that other safe adults can recognize. However, like with most things, this can differ per family.

Decorating Eggs

Speaking of eggs, decorating them is an age-old tradition for the start to spring. I am lucky enough to have parents with chickens, so getting eggs is just a matter of going to their house. You can either clean the eggs out or you can boil them. I have done both, and I personally feel that boiling them is much easier.

If you want to clean them out, use a nail or push pin to poke a hole in each end, then gently blow the contents into a bowl to be used later for cakes or scrambled eggs. Wash them out with water and then set them in an egg carton to dry. I like to cut up the carton to make a little stand. Use a white crayon to draw magic symbols first, because when you dip the egg into the dye, it will not stick to the waxy areas drawn on by the crayon. You can fashion an egg dipper with some copper wire, which works as a great conductor for any magical working, as well. If you have a talent for painting, acrylic paint does the trick, too. You can then thread ribbon through the hole to hang the eggs or cover a toilet paper roll with paper, ribbons, or just paint it, to work as a DIY egg stand.

There are a number of crafts you can make with your kids to honor the rabbit. I have made rabbit ears out of pipe cleaners. I have cut rabbit shapes out of cloth, sewn it together, and let my son pack it with fluffy stuffing. Then we add herbs and crystals, making a spring poppet for wealth, good luck, and as an offering for the goddess. On the day of Ostara, I fill plastic eggs with little toys, bits of paper with good-luck charms, and chocolate coins. My son is so cute with his basket as he goes around the house finding the eggs.

May 1

Beltane is a day that we celebrate fertility of the earth, for humans, animals, and plants alike. Beltane means "bright fire," and we honor the bright fire of creativity, art, science, and life, in general. It marks the beginning of planting season and is a notoriously sexy holiday. It used to be celebrated by coupling, and children conceived on Beltane were considered lucky. So, how do we celebrate such a day with the kids? Easy! Take advantage of the energy to introduce "the birds and the bees," but I will share some other ways to celebrate this bright, festive holiday with your little witchlings.

At Beltane, the veil is as thin as it is on Samhain. It is said to be a day that the Fae travel out of their winter homes and move into their summer homes. My son and I love welcoming our good neighbors back by constructing a faerie altar outside. We collect pretty rocks, shiny trinkets, make little faerie garden accessories (i.e., clay flowers, clay lamp posts, clay faerie houses), and put them around the altar. I then lay down the offering stone - a flat stone depicting the sun and moon - upon which we lay the first offering of the season: a cup of milk and honey (or maple syrup), some cookies (homemade), and sometimes a lollipop from my son.

While helping to make an altar and leave offerings is fine, I must urge you to tell your kids never to attempt to contact the Fae on their own. And to never, under any circumstance, leave with them. Fae are not human, and their idea of funny, such as making you lose your way in the woods, may feel cruel to us.

Morgan Daimler is one of the foremost experts on Fae in the Pagan world today, and I am lucky to have met her. She told me that she tells her kids what is safe and what is not. She advised that I do the same. I talked to her about what my son calls our "good neighbors," elves, because it made me nervous. I never told him to call them that, and I know it is always best to use euphemisms when referring to Fae. She explained that they likely told him that is what they are so he would not be afraid. Daimler told me that it was safe as long as he understood that they are not playmates to follow into the woods.

FLoWer FuN

There are so many flower-themed activities you can do with your kids! You can paint flowers on canvas, draw them on paper, get window markers and draw flowers overlooking the backyard or on a mirror in your living room. My son and I made flower collages last year, cutting pictures out of my stack of *Better Homes and Gardens*. We hung the collage above the altar, which we then decorated with fake ivy and dried flowers to draw the energy of spring into our home and into our magics.

The flower-themed activity I am going to share with you is one that Ember Grant discusses in *Llewellyn's 2020 Sabbats Almanac*, which entails decoupaging pressed flowers.

What you will need:

- Fresh flowers and leaves

- 1-2 pieces of paper (or paper towels)

- Mod Podge glue

- Glass jars and/or decorative landscape stones

There are two ways to press flowers:

- *Old-school method:* Lay a piece of plain paper down in the middle of a big book, arrange the flower or leaf, then lay another piece of paper over it. Close the book. Put a few heavy books on top, and it will be dry in 10 to 14 days. The flower's juices are released, so do not use a book you care about. An old phone book is a great option. Or, put paper towels between the pages and the paper sandwiching the flower.

- *Quick-and-easy method*: Put a paper towel down in your microwave, then a piece of paper. Arrange the flower or leaf and place another paper on top, followed by another paper towel. Then, place a microwave-safe plate, bowl, or mug on top—the heavier the better. Microwave for thirty seconds, then check on it. If it is not fully dry, repeat for another thirty seconds. Repeat until the flower is completely dry and pressed. It should only take a couple of sessions in the microwave.

To decoupage pressed flowers, use tweezers to carefully peel the flower or leaf off the paper, then lay it on a glass jar how you like, or on top of a decorative landscaping stone. Slather Mod Podge on top using the paint brush. Be sure to follow the directions on the bottle regarding how many layers, dry time, and such. When the Mod Podge dries, you have pretty stones or jars! You can place in your garden, use them as paperweights, or as a simple decoration. If using a jar for candles, make sure the jar is candle-safe.

Put On a Play

Beltane celebrates a time in which the ancient Irish Celts ran their cattle and other pasture animals through balefires to gain blessings from the sun god Bel before they went to pasture. You can recreate this with your kids! You will need cardboard, paint, and lots of felt. Cut the cardboard into flame shapes and let your kids paint them to look like fire. Using a staple gun or duct tape, stick the shapes together into two big cardboard "balefires." Put them in your yard or clear a space in the living room so you can have room for the balefires and your kids, who will use the felt to make cow costumes!

As you are making the costumes and balefires, you can tell them about Bel, what the ancient Celts did on Beltane, and why. They learn about the day, have a blast, and get to be creative. Then let your kids be the cows. Encourage them to come up with a fun dance to do as they walk down the path to the cardboard fires. Or they can race each other to the balefires. You could all jump the balefires to rid yourselves of any illness associated with winter and gain blessings from Bel.

The May Queen versus the Winter Queen

Teach your kids about the Wiccan myth of the battle between the May Queen and the Winter Queen. Stacey M. Porter describes them in "Stepping into the Light", in *Llewellyn's 2018 Sabbats Almanac*. She says that the Winter Queen is the wizened old crone, who brings death and grief. She is associated with the dark, the cold, and the frozen heart. The May Queen is queen of the faeries, goddess of flowers, and is associated with new life, youthfulness, and innocence. She brings fertility, love, and light. The Winter Queen has ruled since Samhain and battles the May

Queen for control of the year. She loses to the May Queen on Beltane. And so the world grows warm, colorful, and bright.

Feel free to embellish the story with your kids. Write out lines and character descriptions. Let the creativity flow. If you only have boys you could change "queen" to "king." By putting on a play, your kids will get to act out the changes the world goes through as the season shifts from winter to spring.

FaMiLy RituaL

Rituals and traditions provide the framework for devotional practices. Including your kids in their preparation and performance helps them create their own definitions of what spirituality is and what it means to them. It gives them the tools to develop devotional practices of their own.

Plan the ritual as a family. Get a whiteboard or a notebook. Each member will share what spring means to them. Record everything. For example, spring means renewal to me, playtime to my son, and transformation to my nephew. So, our ritual will include themes of renewal, enjoyment, and change. The ritual should be authentic, and every member should contribute, even the little ones. My son plays just as much a part as any adult.

Preparation for ritual is almost as important as the ritual itself. Rise with the sun, venture out in your PJs and slippers and wash your face with the morning dew. Do some relaxation exercises, like a family yoga session. When the sun is high in the sky, have a lunch made from fresh spring vegetables and fruit, or some fresh-caught fish. Spend some time alone, journaling or reflecting on what you wish to leave behind from the winter, to melt with the last of the frost.

When you are prepared, body and mind, carry out your family ritual. As the sun sets, bring your offerings to the Fae. Since the veil is thin, perform divination, seeking advice from your ancestors, whether of blood or culture. When the moon rises high in the sky, go outside and gaze at the stars. Finally, give thanks.

June 21

The summer solstice, or Litha, is around June 21. The summer solstice is directly opposite the winter solstice on the Wheel of the Year. While the winter solstice marks the longest night, the summer solstice is the longest day. Each season generates a unique energy, which we utilize in our magical practice. Teaching our kids about the summer solstice and enlightening them about all the gifts it has to offer will establish a foundation of practices they can build upon.

The simplest way to celebrate the summer solstice is to take your kids on somewhere outside, like a playground. I most strongly associate the elements of fire and water with summer, so I like to spend the day at the beach. Or you can have a picnic and take time to smell the flowers. While you are having fun, make sure to send thanks up to the sun for this glorious season, and down to the earth for all she provides during this time of year.

Another activity you can do is to go on a nature walk. If you want to make things interesting, make it an *elemental* nature walk. Before you set out, choose an element to focus on. For instance, look for ways that water is manifested. Is there a stream cutting through the woods? Is there dew on a leaf? Are there any puddles where squirrels can stop for a drink, or a bird can sit and splash? Bring a notebook, and as your kids point out water, you can jot down what they say. Asking your kids questions is the best way to trick them into learning about something.

For example, instead of telling your kids to sit by the stream and connect to its spirit, tell them to kick off their shoes and stick their feet in. Then ask them what they think the water's story is. What has the water seen? What is the water's favorite time of day? Who is its best friend? Tell them to silently ask the water these questions and then let you know what it says.

By asking questions that require them to put their creative thinking caps on, you are helping them to shift into a higher brain wave frequency. Encouraging them to connect with the water, you are also training and honing their psychic abilities. What kid would forget about the time their mom or dad had them talk to nature?

Scavenger hunts are another way to kick up the nature walk a notch. I love doing scavenger hunts with my son. He is so competitive and excited when he has the chance to win at anything. Before going out for our walk,

I write down and draw doodles of several things for my son to find. If you have more kids, then you may want to include more items or make it a rule that everyone has to find an item before moving onto the next. Examples of things to list on the scavenger hunt could be trees (specify species for older kids), certain animals, rocks of a certain size or color . . . the possibilities are endless! One of the best scavenger hunts I ever had with my son was when I included "walking stick" on the list. We each found a perfect walking stick, and when we got home, we sanded them down and decorated them. I added protective symbols, bells, and other charms. The next time we set out we were protected spiritually, and less likely to trip (my son trips over his own shadow, and unfortunately it does not matter if he has got a walking stick or not).

August 1

The beginning of August brings the traditional start of the harvest season, known as Lughnasadh. It is also a reminder of the impending end of summer. Luckily, your family is going to make the most of it. There are so many wonderful ways to give your little witchlings an educational, enlightening, and magical summer. While I have yet to hear of a kid who does not have fun casting spells, our little witches need to learn that magic is not only spells. Magic happens everywhere, all the time, for anyone who welcomes it.

Your kids can start summer as little witchlings and return to school in the fall as wise witches. Sure, they will be a little younger and a little shorter than most witches, but age means nothing—it is experience and wisdom that counts.

DIY Bird Feeder

What you will need:

- Jute, string, or yarn.
- Scissors.
- Pine cones. Collect them from your yard. Make it a game: whoever gathers three pine cones first wins!

- Paper plates and a bowl.
- Bird seed.

What you will do:

83

- Using a spoon or a spatula, scoop some peanut butter into the bowl. Start small, so if you need more you can add more. It is better to add more to the bowl than to waste peanut butter. By putting the peanut butter in the bowl first, you do not have to worry about dirt or bits of pine cone getting into the peanut butter jar.

- Then smear peanut butter on the pine cone.

- Place your peanut butter covered pine cone onto the paper plate, then sprinkle bird seed all over it. Another way to do this is to pour birdseed onto the plate and roll the pine cone in it. Whichever method you choose is fine. Your goal is to totally cover the pine cone with bird seed.

- Cut a length of jute or string and tie one end to the pine cone, then tie the pine cone to a tree branch.

DIY Mini-Megaliths

Teach your kids about Stonehenge, telling them about how the sun lines up with key rocks on the solstices. Then make your own mini-megaliths!

What you will need:

- Either several small rocks or clay. If you are opting to use clay, have your kids roll and shape bits of clay into rock-shaped pieces. Follow packaging instructions regarding drying.

- Cardboard.

- Scissors or craft knife.

- Floral moss.

- Ruler.

- Tacky glue, rubber cement, or hot glue gun and hot glue sticks.

- Optional:

◊ *Paint for decorating.*

◊ *Tin can, if you want a pedestal.*

What you will do:

- If you opted to use clay rocks, paint them and let them dry. Tip: use acrylic paint, as it will be dry by the time you are finished with the next steps.

- With the drawing of the design for reference, place the cardboard as a base. Help your kids cut the board into a square big enough for the rock circle.

- With the ruler and pencil, draw a line from the top left corner to the bottom right, and then from the top right to the bottom left. The center of the board is where the lines intersect. Use your pencil to make a big dot so the kids can easily see where the center is if they want the rock circle in the center of the board.

- Have them arrange the rocks around the board per their design to make sure it will all fit and look how they imagined.

- If they are happy with their design, they can glue the rocks to the board.

- Paint some glue all over the board around the rocks and then lay down the moss.

- Optional: If you want to make a little pedestal for the rock structure, clean out an empty tin can. Remove the label and have your kids paint it. When the rocks are secured to the board, you can attach it to the can with more glue.

DIY Summer
Magic Scrapbook

This book is where you will write down all of your magical adventures from the summer, your witchy crafts, spiritually awakening walks, or trips to beaches and parks. If it was magical, put it in the book. Do not just write about it, though. Have your kids draw pictures and slide them into the page protectors. They can stick bits of found nature onto their drawings, like leaves or a flower petal they picked up off the ground, and to the pages. On days you are all cooped up in the house because a thunderstorm is raging outside, you can take out the book to reminisce and feel grateful for the days the weather was great while you write up a list of things you plan to do when the storm passes.

Get a three-ring binder, a package of page protectors, and a stack of lined loose-leaf paper. Decorate the cover. With some Mod Podge you can decoupage pictures onto the cover —either drawn or cut from magazines—or you can use hot glue to attach fabric to the outside. If your kids are old enough to sew, work with them to make a quilted book cover. Sew scrap fabric together to make a rectangle big enough to fit around the photo album (measure when the book is closed, because if you do it open the fabric will be too short). You want your mini quilt to be an inch longer and taller than the book, so you can fold the fabric around the edges and glue it to the binder. It keeps the quilt from getting pulled off and gives the inside of the book a nice colorful border.

The Pick-It-Up Project

I think this makes for a really peaceful way to end the summer. Go out with your family to pick up litter. Your kids get to clean up the land before leaves fall and before they are back to spending their days in school.

Get a map of your town (Google Maps will give you a free satellite image) and print it out. Circle the public places where you know people gather—there is bound to be trash littering the place, and you will not have to worry about trespassing. Put together a trash-picking package. This will be a duffle bag or box where you will keep your bright orange reflector vests, heavy-duty garden gloves, thick-soled shoes, and grabber sticks. If you do not have a grabber stick, a ski pole works, or find a stick in the woods and whittle one end to a point, so you can pick things up without using your hands. If you have a little tool bag or gardening basket, you can repurpose it to hold all the stuff you will need for your litter-picking days, such as sunscreen, bug spray, water bottles, sunglasses, hats . . . you get the idea.

Take time to make sure your kids know how to identify poisonous plants and critters to avoid, as well as trash to leave alone, e.g., animal carcasses, car batteries, hypodermic needles. If you go to www.Earth911.com, they have helpful information on organizing a litter-picking event. They even offer tips and tricks like bringing multiple bags and color coding them so you can keep the litter sorted (plastics, glass, etc.).

As witches, we have a special connection to the earth, and the same goes for your kids. They will care more about the land upon which they live if they take time to tend to it. Their sense of responsibility and environmental awareness will be fostered by the Pick-It-Up Project, and nature will be grateful to your whole family for your help.

September 21

The Autumn Equinox, or Mabon, is often referred to as the witch's Thanksgiving because of feasting and gratitude. We covered gratitude extensively in earlier chapters, but now is the time to make sure your family is staying on top of their gratitude practices. At dinner, or before bed, have your children share something they are grateful for. Some ideas to get them started could be to choose an interaction they had that day, such as, "One thing that happened to me today that I'm grateful for is…" or "I'm grateful for my friend ___ because they said ____ and it made me feel good."

October 31–November 1

For some witches, October 31 is the sacred day of Samhain. Not all witches practice Samhain, but almost all cultures practice some form of appreciation for the dead during this season and many witches will word with spirits/ancestors/their dead in some way. But for most kids, they are focused on the same thing every other kid in America is—Halloween, particularly dressing up and going trick-or-treating.

We could pretend Halloween is just for the mundane, insisting our kids participate in rituals and silent suppers and trying to contact long-dead ancestors. It would certainly teach our little witchlings about Samhain practices, but would probably make them upset with us. What kid would be happy to eat supper in silence with a ghost at the head of the table instead of pretending to be a ghost and filling a sack with candy? We do not want our kids to resent our practices and certainly do not want to alienate them from their friends. But we also do not want to disregard our lifestyle and traditions because our kids learned about Halloween from a classmate or Hollywood.

The solution? Do both! Samhain can be celebrated the entire season of autumn, but trick-or-treating is only one night a year. We can bring our kids the best of both worlds.

Here are some activities you can do as a family:

- Watch Halloween movies.

- Tell Samhain myths while you are sitting around the hearth (or the TV displaying a crackling fire).

- Have a silent supper, or story supper, during which you tell stories of ancestors.

- Apply magic to sewing and crafts to make costumes so you can trick-or-treat witch style.

Many witches may have their reservations about letting their little witchlings go trick-or-treating. Halloween makes a mockery of much of our lifestyle, so why let our kids partake? Learning how trick-or-treating came to be will help you see that it is not far from the ancient practices that provide the foundation of our craft. We mimic the witches of old using cauldrons and besoms, herbs and oils, and establishing traditions that ancient wise folk once took part in. Telling your little witchlings why people started dressing up and asking their neighbors for goodies can be a fun and entertaining way to kick off your costume project. Keep it short and simple, going into a bit more detail as your little witchlings grow every year and can understand more difficult concepts.

While we are not sure where the term "trick or treat" came from, we do know that the custom was firmly established in American pop culture by 1951, when a *Peanuts* comic strip depicted Charlie and the gang trick-or-treating. Then in 1952, Disney produced a cartoon, "Trick or Treat," featuring Donald Duck and his nephews, Huey, Dewey, and Louie. That episode can also be seen in Disney's animated film *Mickey's House of Villains*, which features Halloween-themed shorts.

Trick-or-treating as we know it today comes to us from an assortment of practices that have evolved over the years, the earliest of which date back to the Iron Age in pre-Christian Europe, especially among Celts. Samhain was the most sacred of holidays for the Celts and one of the most terrifying times of the year.

The veil separating the realms of the living and the dead becomes so thin during Samhain that spirits and creatures of the otherworld can easily slip through. While some spirits that come back are good—deities, benevolent Fae, ancestors—some are downright nasty. When the Celts dominated Europe, their very livelihood depended on the success of the harvests (as for all ancient ancestors). While an encounter with a malevolent spirit today would be frightening and might result in a slew of bad luck, it meant failed crops in the Iron Age. In hopes of avoiding encounters with malevolent spirits, Celts would disguise themselves using animal skins. They thought that the spirit or creature would just pass by if they did not know it was a human they encountered.

It was during the Middle Ages when this act of disguising oneself shifted. Instead of using animal skins to hide from evil ghosts and monsters, people started the tradition of "mumming." They would dress as scary as possible—as ghosts, goblins, and ghouls—and would perform tricks and put on shows in exchange for food and drink.

In 1000 CE, the church designated November 2, as All Souls' Day, the Christian equivalent of Samhain, as it was a time to honor the dead.

They had bonfires and masquerades that drew Pagans into the church. Poor people would trek into wealthy neighborhoods and go door-to-door, promising to pray for the homeowners' dead relatives if the wealthy family gave them "soul cakes."

As time went on, children took over the practice, calling it "souling." They would not only accept soul cakes, but would take the opportunity to beg for money, food, and other treats. In Ireland and Scotland, young people took part in "guising," too. They dressed up in costumes and accepted offerings of fruit, nuts, or coins from households after performing poetry, songs, jokes, or some other trick.

As people from these cultures eventually came to America, they brought their practices with them. Others adopted the traditions, each generation adding its own flair until it became what we all know and love today: trick-or-treating.[46]

Create Your OWN Costume

Creating a Pagan-themed costume will most certainly give you an opportunity to teach your kids about the lore and legends of Samhain. If your kids are into superheroes and fantasy novels, share with them some Celtic myths associated with Samhain. The myths may inspire them to turn Dagda or the Morrigan into a costume, allowing them to think of the deities as real-life superheroes. The myths may also inspire them to choose a magical creature to dress as, such as a pookah, banshee, or Fae.

Perhaps you share with them a story about an ancestor you admire. Your kids could dress as the ghost of that ancestor. If you tell your kids that your Samhain spiritual practices are being carried out in part to help them come up with the perfect costume, they will definitely be more enthusiastic about participating. The ideas do not even have to come from Samhain-related myths. Any myth or legend that aligns with your lifestyle will do. I rely on books on mythological creatures and use Google and Pinterest to come up with ideas.

---

46   History.com Editors "How Trick-or-Treating Became a Halloween Tradition" History.com, Updated Oct. 25, 2021, https://www.history.com/news/halloween-trick-or-treating-origins

Here is a list of suggestions to get you started:

- Dragons.

- Faeries.

- Mermaids.

- Ghosts.

- Animals and beings that represent the zodiac.

- Sacred or magical animals like the crow, owl, dog, wolf, salmon, bear, or deer.

- Representations of the elements (for kid themed ideas, watch *Frozen II*).

By choosing a unique costume idea, you are left with the potential downside of not being able to walk into your local superstore and pick a costume off the rack. But that does not have to be a problem! By making your costume at home, you are provided the opportunity to teach your kids how to put magic into their crafts, in addition to life skills like sewing. They can stitch spells into capes and caps, enchant costume jewelry, or paint sigils on the inside of hats and shoe-covers, fusing magic into their costume.

Have your kids think long and hard about something they want to manifest. When they have their idea, tell them to write down what they want in a short sentence that will serve as their intention. Help the little ones with theirs, but let your older kids keep their intention to themselves. This will teach them the importance of the witch rule of secrecy - by keeping the intention to yourself, the energy remains focused on manifesting the desire.

By using simple correspondence charts, going by colors and shapes, you can turn the costume into a wearable spell. You can use materials like felt, fabric, yarn, ribbon, paint, cardboard, construction paper—things you probably have around the house. Pinterest and Google will be excellent resources on step-by-step instructions for ways to make dresses, animal bodies, and accessories like a mermaid tails or fairy wings.

These costumes do not have to be ritually charged, either. The time, thought, and energy put into making the costume will be more than enough to fuse the energy needed to manifest the desire. As your little ones go door to door all around the neighborhood, they are releasing the energy into the universe.

When they get home they can each pick one piece of candy to use as an offering. They can give it to the spirit of the animal they dressed as, to ancestors, or to the magical being they emulated that night. This helps to create a foundation of devotional and magical practice for them.

FINAL THOUGHTS

There are a number of ways to instill a foundation of spirituality in our children, giving them boundaries to make them feel safe and freedom to determine their own beliefs. I believe that deities, and other powers that be, choose the human to work with. It is for this reason that I will not talk to my son about specific entities. I know that they will go to him when he is ready. And should he choose, he will have the skills and tools to communicate and work with them in a safe, rewarding manner. Spiritual practices entail the use of magic and divination for witches, which is why I put this chapter last. It is probably the most important, but it takes a culmination of learning, practice, and dedication to carry out.

Chapter 7

PRACTICING PARENTHOOD

"We all fail Mum School, sometimes...
We can just start again tomorrow."

- CHILI, *BLUEY*

OFTEN THINK OF PARENTHOOD AS A practice. It is something you are constantly learning, striving to improve, and never-ending. Likewise, your practice will never be perfect, but there is always growth – just like parenthood. Since I began to think of parenting as a practice, I have found that I am not quite so hard on myself when I mess up with Josh. I know I will never be perfect. There is no such thing. All I can do is learn, and explore, maybe experiment a bit, and keep striving to improve.

You have just been on a journey, breaking down your spiritual and magical practices to thoroughly evaluate what you do, why you do it, and then share that practice with your kids. As you have learned, however, it is important to take your child's interests, passions, and skills into consideration when laying the foundations of their practice. There may be roads they will be thrilled to travel down that you never knew existed. Or you are well aware, but uninterested. Combining the fundamental values and traditions of your practices with the passions, interests, and predispositions of your children helps to establish the foundation of a practice upon which your child will build as they grow into adulthood.

These short and sweet chapters have likely become your best friends by now, as the contents have proven useful as you adjusted your parenting approach and figured out how you want to raise your little witchlings.

LITTLE WITCHLING LITERATURE AND LEARNING

This list is a combination of fiction and nonfiction for little witchlings. I organized the list based on the listed reading age (per Amazon), going from youngest to oldest.

Reading age: 4-8

- *The Adventures of Little Laveau*, Erin Rovin (Pelican Publishing, 2018).

    ◊ *Book 1: A Magical Bedtime Story*

    ◊ *Book 2: Bayou Beware*

    ◊ *Book 3: Pirate Adventure*

- *Tutty Learns About Witches*, Tonya A. Brown (Witch Way Publishing, 2021).

- *A Kid's Herb Book: For Children of All Ages*, Lesley Tierra (Robert Reed Publishers, 2018).

- *The Magic of Me*, Becky Cummings (Boundless Movement Inc, 2019).

    ◊ *My Magical Words*

    ◊ *My Magical Choices*

    ◊ *My Magical Dreams*

    ◊ *My Magical Gifts*

    ◊ *My Magical Foods*

◊ *My Magical Feelings*

- *Aidan's First Full Moon Circle*, W. Lyon Martin (Magical Child Books, 2008).

- *An Ordinary Girl, A Magical Child*, W. Lyon Martin (Magical Child Books, 2008).

Reading Age: 8-12

- *Tarot for Kids* (deck and guidebook), Theresa Reed (Sounds True, 2021).

- *The Little Witch's Book of Spells*, Ariel Kusby (Chronicle Books, 2020).

- *The Junior Handbook*, Nikki Van De Car (Running Press Kids).

    ◊ *The Junior Witches Handbook (2020)*

    ◊ *The Junior Astrologers Handbook (2021)*

Reading Age 13+

- *Elements of Witchcraft: Nature Magick for Teens*, Ellen Dugan (Llewellyn Publications, 2003).

- *Teen Magick: Witchcraft for a New Generation*, Fiona Horne (Rockpool Publishing, 2021).

- *Teen Witch: Wicca for a New Generation*, Silver Ravenwolf (Llewellyn Publications, 1998).

- *The Witch's Vacuum Cleaner and Other Stories*, Terry Pratchett (HarperCollins, 2017).

RESOURCES FOR PARENTS

Refer to the bibliography for a full list of resources, but the following books and websites have been particularly helpful in my journey as a witch parent.

- Llewellyn's Witches' Companions

- Llewellyn's Magical Almanacs

- Llewellyn's Sabbats Almanacs

- *Parenting Pagan Tots*, Janet Callahan

- *Psychic Witch: A Metaphysical Guide to Meditation, Magick, & Manifestation*, Mat Auryn

- *Circle Round: Raising Children in Goddess Traditions*, Starhawk, Anne Hill and Diane Baker

- *The Door to Witchcraft: A New Witch's Guide to History, Traditions, & Modern-Day Spells*, Tonya Brown

- *Buckland's Complete Book of Witchcraft*, Ray Buckland

- *The Magickal Family: Pagan Living in Harmony with Nature*, Monica Crosson

- *The Magical Household*, Scott Cunningham

- *Witchy Mama: Magickal Traditions, Motherly Insights, and Sacred Knowledge*, E. Francis and M. Marquis

- *Nurturing Spirituality in Children*, Penny Jenkins

- *Children of the Green: Raising Our Kids in Pagan Traditions*, Hannah Johnston

- *The Pregnant Goddess: Your Guide to Traditions, Rituals, and Blessings for a Sacred Pagan Pregnancy*, Arin Murphy-Hiscock

- magickalmamas.com

- Parenting.com

- Parents.com

- circlesanctuary.org

- thetravelingwitch.com

- patheos.com

- habitsforwellbeing.com

- Paganfederation.org

- moodymoons.com

FINAL THOUGHTS

There are many resources out there, you just have to be open to their advice. I know it is not easy to seek help. Trust me, I am a Taurus, so I know how hard it is. But it is actually wonderful to learn something new. It is even better to learn that you have been doing something right. Just think of parenting as a practice.

Like witchcraft, parenting is not going to be a perfect, complete thing. It has a life of its own that grows, matures, evolves, and changes. It will take on a personality of its own once you have found your rhythm. When your kids start meeting milestones and goals and thank you for being their parent, then you will know you are doing great.

Conclusion

"Done properly, parenting is a heroic act."

—EDNA MODE, *THE INCREDIBLES 2* (2018)

PARENTING GIVES YOU A SENSE OF purpose and pride. At the same time, it fills you with doubt and paralyzing fear. Parenting is difficult. Parenting is exhausting. Parenting is messy as hell and can be frustrating beyond belief. Looking at your children brings to your attention the very blood flowing through your veins. The involuntary contractions of your lungs draw in air so you can live *for them.* Everything you do, everything you say, or even think, can be tied back to them. They are your life. It does not matter how they came to be yours. What matters is that they are yours. And that responsibility is incredible.

We are bound to stumble sometimes. I once got a call from the school. My son's aid called to tell me that he was having a "difficult" day. He had a melt down and threw a couple of chairs at his teacher. *He threw chairs.* And the aid said, "it's not that bad!" Yes, actually, I thought, that is incredibly bad! It is so bad that tears of frustration, embarrassment, and self-doubt started streaming down my face. But later that day, when Josh came home, I overheard him talking to his baby brother. It went something like, "Don't cry, Logan, Brother is here. Brother will never let anything bad happen to you. Brother loves you. Brother will teach you how to do stuff, like play with clay

99

and brush your teeth...when you get teeth. Hey Mommy? When will Logan have teeth?" And just like that, I was back to being the proud parent. I went from feeling as if I was a failure because of my son's outburst, to feeling pride in his kindness. All in the same day.

Parenting is like that. It is full of these magical and magnificent memories. There will be times when we get it wrong- sometimes horribly wrong - but, as Chili from the animated show, *Bluey*, says, "We can just start again tomorrow."

As witches, we have chosen an approach to parenting that may be more difficult, yet also more rewarding. It will be gratifying because if we get it even half right, our kids will grow into people who are intuitive and empathetic, who look at their life and see opportunity. They will love themselves and take nothing for granted. They will know their potential and their place in the world, and will seek to play a role that not only benefits them, but those around them. They will know and appreciate the magic of the world, take time to look up at the moon and stars, to close their eyes and feel a warm spring rain, to just sit and listen to the summer morning birdsong.

Learning the craft will not always be fun or easy, but we will do our best to make it as exciting and intriguing as possible. We will show them how to read Tarot, teach them how to charm a meal, and encourage them to trust their instincts so they can interpret symbols sent from Spirit. And we will learn right along with them. We will gain an understanding of the world that can only be taught by an innocent child.

It has been an incredible journey so far, and I am honored and grateful to have the opportunity to share it with you. It is my most sincere hope that you will make this material your own, and raise your little witchlings with love, patience, and pride. From my family to yours, thank you!

ABOUT THE AUTHOR

AMANDA WILSON, artist, witch, & SAHM strives to maintain balance between motherhood, witchcraft, and her blossoming career. Amanda's career is an amalgamation of duties: Columnist and Submissions Manager for *Witch Way Magazine*; executive assistant for The *Witch Daily Show* podcast; and content creator, contributing to Medium.com, Vocal.Media, and Hubpages.com. (It's no wonder she is passionate about planners!) To access online profiles or view her writing works, visit Amanda's author's website,

www.WriteKindofMagic.art.

Bibliography

"7 Simple Beltane Activities with your Kids." Magickal Mamas
 Blog. January 1, 2017. http://magickalmamascom/7-simple-
 beltane-activities-with-kids/

"Assertiveness." Wikipedia. Last modified March 30, 2022. https://
 en.wikipedia.org/wiki/Assertiveness

Allen, Summer. *The Science of Gratitude*. Berkeley: John Templeton
 Foundation, 2018. https://ggsc.berkeley.edu/images/uploads/
 GGSC-JTF_White_Paper-Gratitude-FINAL.pdf

Auryn, Mat. *Psychic Witch: A Metaphysical Guide to Meditation, Magick,
 & Manifestation*. Woodbury: Llewellyn Publications, 2020.

Baker, Diane, Ann Hill, and Starhawk. *Circle Round: Raising Children
 in Goddess Traditions*. New York: Bantam Books, 2000. Kindle.

Basile, Lisa Marie. *Magical Writing Grimoire: Use the Word as Your Wand
 for Magic, Manifestation & Ritual*. Beverly: Fair Winds Press,
 2020. Kindle.

Blake, Debra. "Worshipping Widely and Cultural Appropriation". In
 Llewellyn's 2018 Witches' Companion, edited by Andrea Neff, 34-
 40. Woodbury: Llewellyn Publications, 2017.

Brown, Tonya. *The Door to Witchcraft: A New Witch's Guide to History, Traditions,
 & Modern-day Spells*. Emeryville: Althea Press, 2019. Kindle.

Buckland, Raymond. *Buckland's Complete Book of Witchcraft*. Woodbury:
 Llewellyn Publications, 2017.

Callahan, Janet. *Parenting Pagan Tots*. Self-published, 2015. Kindle.

Cettina, Teri. "Teaching Spirituality to Kids." Parenting. December 19, 2010.
 https://www.parenting.com/child/teach-spirituality-kids/

"Child and Adolescent Psychology". Lumen Learning Courses. Florida State College at Jacksonville. Accessed February 22, 2022. https://courses.lumenlearning.com/atd-fscj-childpsychology/chapter/self-awareness-and-identity-development/

Christy. "Wheel of the Year: Beltane." Wayward Inspiration. Last modified April 22, 2021. https://waywardinspiration.com/beltane/

Crosson, Monica. *The Magickal Family: Pagan Living in Harmony with Nature*. Woodbury: Llewellyn Publications, 2017. Kindle.

Crosson, Monica. "Under a Blood Moon: A Family Ritual." In *Llewellyn's 2017 Witches' Companion*, edited by Ed Day, 175-86. Woodbury: Llewellyn Publications, 2016. Kindle.

Crowther, Susan, and Jennifer Hall. "Spirituality and Spiritual Care in and Around Childbirth." *Women and Birth*, 23, no. 2, (2015):173-178. https://doi.org/10.1016j.wombi.2015.01.001.

Cunningham, Scott and David Harrington. *The Magical Household*. Woodbury: Llewellyn Publications, 2016.

Dahl, Roald. "Quote by Roald Dahl." Goodreads. Accessed April 25, 2022. https://www.goodreads.com/quotes/7032-and-above-all-watch-with-glittering-eyes-the-whole-world

Emyme. "Magical Prep for the Nursery." In *Llewellyn's 2020 Witches' Companion*, 218-228. Woodbury: Llewellyn Publications, 2019. Kindle.

Fox, Selena. "Guide to Nature Spirituality Terms". Circle Sanctuary. Accessed February 22, 2022. https://www.circlesanctuary.org/index.php/about-Paganism/guide-to-nature-spirituality-terms

Francis, Emily and Melanie Marquis. (2016). *Witchy Mama: Magickal Traditions, Motherly Insights, and Sacred Knowledge*. Woodbury: Llewellyn Publications, 2016. Kindle.

Grimassi, Raven. *What We Knew in the Night: Reawakening the Heart of Witchcraft*. Red Wheel/Weiser Book, 2019.

History.com Editors. "How Trick-or-Treating Became a Halloween Tradition." History.com. Updated Oct. 25, 2021. https://www. history.com/news/halloween-trick-or-treating-origins

Hortwort, J.D. "Beltane Beyond the Maypole." in *Llewellyn's 2020 Sabbat Almanac*, edited by Annie Burdick, 159- 165. Woodbury: Llewellyn Publications, 2019. Kindle.

Hortwort, J.D. "Imbolc." in *Llewellyn's 2019 Sabbat Almanac*, edited by Aaron Lawrence, Section 3, article 1. Woodbury: Llewellyn Publications, 2018. Kindle.

Iannelli, Vincent. "How Kids Make and Keep Friends." Very Well Family. Last modified July 21, 2021. https://www.verywellfamily. com/making-and-keeping-friends-2633627#toc-why-friendships-are-important

Jane. "What is Personal Accountability?" Habits for Wellbeing. Last modified August 24, 2014. https://www.habitsforwellbeing.com/ what-is-personal-accountability/

Jenkins, Peggy. *Nurturing Spirituality in Children.* New York: Atria Books, 2008. Kindle.

Johnston, Hannah. *Children of the Green: Raising Our Kids in Pagan Traditions.* Washington: Moon Books, 2014. Kindle.

Johnston, Hannah. "From Child to Parent-Growing up in a Pagan Family." Patheos Blog. Last modified January 23, 2014. https:// www.patheos.com/blogs/Paganfamilies/2014/01/from-child-to-parent-growing-up-in-a-Pagan-family/

Jones, Prudence. "What is Paganism?". Pagan Federation International. December 17, 2011. https://www.paganfederation.org/what-is-Paganism.

Meredith, Jane. "Magical kids." In *Llewellyn's 2016 Witches' Companion*, edited by Andrea Neff, 152-160. Woodbury: Llewellyn Publications, 2015. Kindle.

Metcalfe, Tom. "Operation Cone of Power: When British Witches Attacked Adolf Hitler." Mental Floss. October 18, 2016. https://www.mentalfloss.com/article/86145/operation-cone-power-when-british-witches-attacked-adolf-hitler

Murphy-Hiscock, Arin. (2020). *The Pregnant Goddess: Your Guide to Traditions, Rituals, and Blessings for a Sacred Pagan Pregnancy.* New York: Adams Media, 2020. Kindle.

Newman, Catherine. "10 Simple ways to raise a respectful child." Parents. March 19, 2021. https://www.parents.com/parenting/better-parenting/positive/how-to-raise-a-respectful-child/

"Pagan Pregnancy." Moody Moons. Last modified November 20, 2015. https://www.moodymoons.com/2015/11/20/Pagan-pregnancy/.

Porter, Stacy. "Stepping into the Light." In *Llewellyn's 2018 Sabbat Almanac*, edited by Aaron Lawrence, 160-164. Woodbury: Llewellyn Publications, 2017. Kindle.

Ravenwolf, Silver. *To Ride a Silver Broomstick: New Generation Witchcraft.* Woodbury: Llewellyn Publications, 2017.

Rovin, Erin. *Little Laveau: Bayou Beware.* Metairie: River Road Press, 2017.

Schafer, Jack. "Why Keeping Secrets Heightens Anxiety and Depression." Psychology Today. Last modified May 15, 2021. https://www.psychologytoday.com/us/blog/let-their-words-do-the-talking/202105/why-keeping-secrets-heightens-anxiety-and-depression

Scott, Elizabeth. "What is Spirituality." Very Well Mind. Last modified November 27, 2020. https://www.verywellmind.com/how-spirituality-can-benefit-mental-and-physical-health-3144807

Smith, Jeremy Adam. "The Science of the Story." Berkely Blog, Berkely News. Last modified August 25, 2016, https://news.berkeley.edu/berkeley_blog/the-science-of-the-story.

Stephen, Wacuka. "Self-Awareness: Understanding Your Core Identity." Thrive Global. Accessed February 15, 2022. https://thriveglobal.com/stories/self-awareness-understanding-your-core-identity/

Tipton, Melissa. "Unlocking the Magical Power of Polarity." In *Llewellyn's 2019 Witches' Companion*, edited by Andrea Neff, 92-102. Woodbury: Llewellyn Publications, 2018.

Tomaine, Gina. "How to Practice Nature-Based Spirituality Responsibly". Yoga Journal, Accessed February 20, 2022. https://www.yogajournal.com/lifestyle/how-to-practice-nature-based-spirituality-responsibly/

"Treating Children as Individuals." Healthy Children Blog. American Academy of Pediatrics. Last modified November 21, 2015. https://healthychildren.org/English/family-life/family-dynamics/Pages/Treating-Children-as-Individuals.aspx

Tressabelle. "Divination for Kids." Ozark Pagan Mamma Blog. Last modified October 6, 2013. https://tressabelle.wordpress.com/2013/10/06/divination-for-kids/

"The Self and Identity: 5 Ways to Encourage Your Child's Individuality" Parent Resources Blog, KidsAcademy.mobi. Last modified January 23, 2017. https://www.kidsacademy.mobi/storytime/self-and-identity-5-ways-encourage-your-childs-individuality/

Walls, Charlynn. "The Old Ways: Predicting the Weather." In *Llewellyn's 2020 Sabbat Almanac*, edited by Annie Burdick, 97-101. Woodbury: Llewellyn Publications, 2019. Kindle.

Walsh, Froma. "Spiritual Diversity: Multifaith Perspectives in Family Therapy." Family Process, 49, no. 3 (2010): 330-48. DOI: 10.1111/j.1545-5300.2010.01326.x

Wikipedia. "Paganism." Last modified April 25, 2022. https://en.wikipedia.org/wiki/Paganism.

Willis, Judy. "The Neuroscience of Joyful Education." ASCD.com. June 1, 2007. http://www.ascd.org/publications/educational-leadership/summer07/vol64/num09/The-Neuroscience-of-Joyful-Education.aspx

York, Twilia. "Children in the Pagan Community." Huffpost. March 25, 2017. https://www.huffpost.com/entry/children-in-the-pagan community_b_58d54621e4b06c3d3d3e6cff

Zakroff, Laura Tempest. "A Witch's Guide to Essential Etiquette." In *Llewellyn's 2019 Witches' Companion*, edited by Andrea Neff, 38-46. Woodbury, MN: Llewellyn Publications, 2018.

Zakroff, Laura Tempest. *Weave the Liminal: Living Modern Traditional Witchcraft*. Woodbury, MN: Llewellyn Publications, 2019.

CPSIA information can be obtained
at www.ICGtesting.com
Printed in the USA
LVHW080734210822
726390LV00004B/635